CUSTOMER ATTRACTANT

How to Lure The Best Customers & Explode Your Wildlife and Pest Control Revenue

Tate Morgan
President, LeadSquirrel Marketing

All rights reserved. **No portion of this book or document may be reproduced in any form without written permission from the publisher or author,** except as permitted by U.S. copyright law.

TABLE OF CONETNTS

Foreward 1

Part 1: Introduction 3

Chapter 1: Introduction to Digital Marketing for Wildlife Removal and Pest Control Companies 4

Chapter 2: The Customer Attractant™ System for Pest Control & Wildlife Removal Companies 10

Part 2: Creating Your System 16

Chapter 3: Building an Action Plan 17

Chapter 4: Understanding Your Target Audience 20

Part 3: Technical, Tactical Execution 30

Chapter 5: Building an Effective Website 31

Chapter 6: Search Engine Optimization (SEO) 42

Chapter 7: Pay-Per-Click (PPC) Advertising 59

Chapter 8: Social Media Marketing 69

Chapter 9: Content Marketing 80

Chapter 10: Email Marketing 86

Chapter 11: Online Reputation Management 91

Chapter 12: Analytics and Reporting 94

Chapter 13: Empowering Traditional Marketing with Digital Strategies .. 99

Chapter 14: Future Trends in Digital Marketing for Wildlife Removal and Pest Control Companies 102

Chapter 15: Conclusion 104

Appendix: Tools and Resources 106

CUSTOMER ATTRACTANT

FOREWARD

From the Author:
I can't express enough how thankful I am that you are reading this book. My name is Tate Morgan, and I wrote this book to serve as a huge resource for digital marketing for wildlife removal and pest control businesses. The chapters are designed to stand alone. If you want to explore SEO, flip to the SEO chapter. If you want to explore content marketing, jump to the content marketing chapter. You don't have to read this in order. My goal is that no matter where you start, you should find something that benefits your business.

Now for some history.

I have been in the marketing world for over 10 years. I started on the brand side working to scale companies in the hunting industry. After four years working on the brand side, I moved into an ad agency where I worked hands-on with dozens of businesses, growing and developing PPC and SEO campaigns.

In 2020, like so many others, I was laid off due to the COVID-19 pandemic. I'm not the type of person who can sit still, so I reached out to some friends whose businesses were thriving despite the pandemic to see how I could help. With their help and some referrals within their network, I began freelance marketing with 3 pest control companies and a wildlife removal company. This momentum grew into what would eventually become my own agency, LeadSquirrel.

(LeadSquirrel President Tate Morgan speaking at the 2024 NWCOA Wildlife Expo)

So now that we've got the history out of the way, let's address the elephant in the room…

If I own an agency that provides these things as a service, why write a DIY book?

One thing I have learned in the agency world is that there are ALWAYS people who prefer to DIY. As pest and wildlife operators, you know this, too. And sometimes, with the right tools and resources, a DIYer can do a pretty great job.

I want this book to serve as the resource that allows the DIYer to do not just a pretty good job, but a great job. The more you grow, the more the industry grows. The more the industry grows, the more opportunities are created for everyone.

PART 1
INTRODUCTION

CHAPTER 1

Introduction to Digital Marketing for Wildlife Removal and Pest Control Companies

---

Bugs in the System

There's a problem with marketing in the pest and wildlife world — a bug in the system. If you've ever tried to engage with marketing providers for your pest or wildlife removal company, you know exactly what I'm talking about. There are a dozen or so companies (many of which are actually the same company under different names) that claim to help you with your marketing, only to sell you "leads" in the form of unscreened calls. These calls might be looking for your competitors, the dog warden, an animal rescue, or a local government animal control service. These cheap tire-kickers don't provide any value for your business, but you end up paying for the lead anyway.

Then there are the digital marketing agencies. Some do great work, but they aren't well-versed in pest control or wildlife removal, so you've got to hold their hands every step of the way. This results in more time and energy wasted, and if you don't have the time to handhold, you'll end up with cat & dog calls from them too.

This leaves you two options.

Work with a marketing team that actually understands your industry, or do it all yourself. If you find the latter enticing, this book is for you.

The "Tried It" Problem

By now, when you hear about certain marketing channels and tools, you probably think to yourself "I've already tried it." When you're working to grow your business, you try EVERYTHING. Sometimes you find a home run solution, but more often than not, you're left with a ton of money spent and not much to show for it.

The reality is that you're an expert in pest control and wildlife removal, NOT in marketing, and that's OK! When you DIY your marketing strategies, you're putting yourself up against companies who have hired expert employees or expert agencies to do their marketing. It's a tough hill to climb.

But with the right resources, it's not impossible.

The Digital Marketing Solution

Digital marketing has become a crucial aspect for pest control and wildlife removal companies in today's highly competitive business landscape. I cannot stress enough the significance of having a robust digital marketing strategy in place. With the majority of consumers now relying on the internet to search for services, read reviews, and make informed decisions, digital marketing has become the cornerstone of success for pest control and wildlife removal businesses.

One of the primary reasons why digital marketing is essential for this industry is the ability to effectively target and reach the right audience. By utilizing various digital channels such as search engines, social media, and email marketing, companies can strategically target their marketing efforts towards individuals who are actively searching for pest control and wildlife removal services. This targeted approach not only increases the chances of reaching potential customers, but it also allows for more efficient use of marketing resources and budget, resulting in a higher return on investment (ROI).

Digital marketing allows pest control and wildlife removal companies to establish a strong online presence and build brand awareness. A professional website, optimized for search engines, coupled with engaging social media content and positive online reviews, can significantly enhance a company's credibility and reputation. It also provides an avenue for companies to showcase their expertise and educate customers about their services, which can help in building trust and loyalty among customers.

In addition, digital marketing enables companies to engage and interact with their customers in real-time. Through email marketing, social media, and online reviews, companies can communicate directly with their customers, address their queries or concerns, and provide timely updates about their services. This personalized approach not only fosters customer satisfaction but also helps in building long-term relationships with customers, leading to repeat business and positive word-of-mouth referrals.

Channels, Strategies, and the Five Core Pillars

The information contained in this book is the result of helping dozens of wildlife removal and pest control experts grow their businesses. We've found firsthand what works to bring clients to your doorstep.

While there are hundreds of specific marketing channels, platforms, strategies, and concepts that could be considered for your animal removal business, research and experience have pointed to five core areas in which to focus to create a comprehensive marketing strategy.

We call these five segments our Core Marketing Pillars. These are:

1. Paid Search Marketing - Google Ads, Bing Ads, Amazon Alexa Placement, Quora, and Similar Platforms.
2. Paid Social Marketing - Meta (FB/IG) Ads, Nextdoor Advertising, Snap Ads and Geofiltering, and Similar Platforms
3. Organic Search Marketing - Search Engine Optimization, Google Business Profile Listing, Map Pack Placement, Blogging & Content, and Location Definition
4. Organic Social Marketing - Establishing and Maintaining a Presence on the Social Media Platforms that Matter Most for Your Customers
5. Strategic Communication - Email Marketing, Public Relations, and Reputation Management.

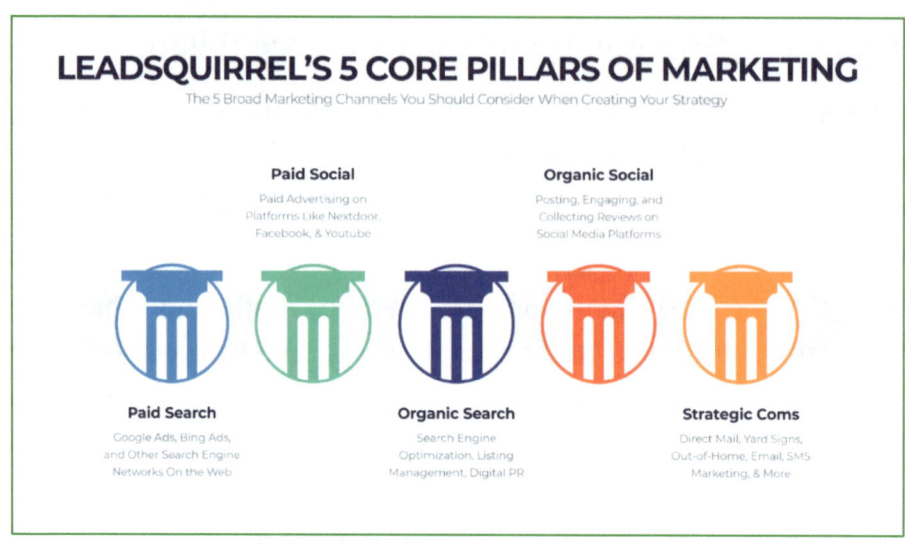

LEADSQUIRREL'S 5 CORE PILLARS OF MARKETING
The 5 Broad Marketing Channels You Should Consider When Creating Your Strategy

Paid Social — Paid Advertising on Platforms Like Nextdoor, Facebook, & Youtube

Organic Social — Posting, Engaging, and Collecting Reviews on Social Media Platforms

Paid Search — Google Ads, Bing Ads, and Other Search Engine Networks On the Web

Organic Search — Search Engine Optimization, Listing Management, Digital PR

Strategic Coms — Direct Mail, Yard Signs, Out-of-Home, Email, SMS Marketing, & More

(LeadSquirrel's 5 Core Pillars of Marketing)

So why do we think in terms of these pillars?

Busy wildlife removal & pest control pros are often skilled operators who are in the field, ready to take any wildlife issues head-on.

That also means that our wildlife & pest experts don't want to think about dozens of marketing channels.

We think about digital marketing for wildlife removal & pest control professionals in terms of pillars because it helps simplify the marketing process AND make digital marketing more accessible.

One last question… Why are the *paid* pillars first?

That's an excellent question. Pest and wildlife professionals want to move toward profitability as quickly as possible. Organic Social and Organic Search are both long-term plays. They're incredibly effective, but a solid strategy around each takes 3-6 months before *real* momentum starts. This can often be demotivating for business owners.

We recommend starting with paid platforms first so tangible progress can be seen as early as possible. We also recommend using paid platform results to inform organic strategies. You can use paid pillars to identify the audience segments or types of content that lead to the most business growth.

CHAPTER 2

The Customer Attractant™ System for Pest Control & Wildlife Removal Companies

---

A Surprise Breakfast Guest

It was the break of dawn, and Jim was awakened from a deep slumber by the excited squeals of his five-year-old daughter, Ellie. His head was still foggy from sleep, but the pitch of his daughter's enthusiasm was enough to shake him out of his drowsiness. Ellie bounced around him, her golden curls shaking with her enthusiastic movements, as she babbled on about a bird in the kitchen.

A bird? In the kitchen? Jim rubbed his eyes, put on his glasses, and headed toward the kitchen, half-expecting to see a feathered friend perched on the kitchen counter. Ellie was a ball of joy behind him, practically radiating excitement.

Upon entering the kitchen, Jim was immediately taken aback. The creature that fluttered around the kitchen wasn't a bird at all—it was

CUSTOMER ATTRACTANT

a bat. He froze in place, eyes wide. Bats were known to carry rabies. This was far from the early morning surprise he would have preferred.

Panic surged through Jim as he ushered Ellie out of the kitchen, instructing her to stay in the living room. The little girl looked up at him with puzzled eyes, the edge of her excitement tempered by her father's serious tone.

With Ellie safely away from the kitchen, Jim reached for his phone, heart still pounding. He fumbled through a quick internet search, trying to find a company that could handle his unexpected bat problem. A flurry of clicks later, he found a local wildlife control company that claimed to specialize in the humane removal of bats.

With a shaky breath, he dialed the number and was immediately greeted by a calm, professional voice. He quickly explained the situation and was relieved when they promised to send a specialist within the hour.

-A quick thanks to Jim Everett of Winston-Salem, NC for sharing this story with us!

(The breakfast that could have been...)

What Can We Learn from Jim's Story?

Jim's experience is all too familiar for many homeowners. When faced with an unexpected wildlife problem, there's no time to waste—people need help, and they need it fast. The first place they turn? The internet.

This is where your company's online presence becomes critical.

Wildlife removal and pest control companies thrive in moments of urgency. Whether it's a bat in the kitchen or squirrels in the attic, customers want to find a solution quickly. A well-built digital marketing system ensures that your business shows up *right when* these potential customers are searching for help.

By leveraging a strategic online presence—one that includes local SEO, paid ads, and a steady flow of customer reviews—you can make sure your business is the one they find first. It's not just about being visible, it's about being *accessible* and trustworthy. When your website is optimized for quick navigation and offers immediate contact options, you create an experience that builds confidence, just like the calm voice that reassured Jim.

Having an integrated digital marketing system ensures that your company is always top-of-mind and easy to find, positioning you as the immediate go-to solution when it matters most.

Components of a Digital Marketing System

While each company's system may vary slightly, a successful digital marketing system for wildlife removal and pest control companies typically includes the following components:

CUSTOMER ATTRACTANT

1. **Website:** This serves as your business's digital hub. It should be user-friendly, mobile-responsive, and populated with relevant, informative content about your services. Highlight your expertise in pest control and wildlife removal, and provide convincing evidence of your proficiency, such as case studies or testimonials.
2. **Search Engine Optimization (SEO):** SEO involves optimizing your website and its content to rank higher on search engine results, thereby increasing your visibility. It includes keyword optimization, link building, and ensuring your website's speed and performance are up to par.
3. **Content Marketing:** This involves creating valuable content such as blog posts, infographics, and videos that provide useful information about pest control and wildlife removal. This not only improves your SEO ranking but also establishes you as an authority in your field.
4. **Social Media Marketing:** Platforms like Facebook, Instagram, and Twitter can serve as additional channels for engaging with your audience. Share your content, interact with followers, and use these platforms for customer service.
5. **Email Marketing:** This enables you to maintain communication with your customers by sending them regular updates, tips, and offers. This can help nurture leads, improve customer retention, and encourage referrals.
6. **Online Advertising:** Pay-per-click (PPC) advertising or social media ads can provide a significant boost to your online visibility. These can be targeted to your specific demographic and geographic areas to ensure your ads reach the most relevant audience.

7. **Analytics and Reporting:** This component involves monitoring and analyzing your digital marketing efforts to understand what's working and what's not. Use tools like Google Analytics to track your performance and make data-driven decisions.

Lead Tracking & CRM Integration

Integrating lead tracking with a Customer Relationship Management (CRM) system, such as Salesforce or HubSpot, can significantly enhance your ability to manage customer relationships and improve follow-up processes. By capturing and organizing leads in one place, you gain insights into the entire customer journey—from initial inquiry to service completion. CRMs allow you to automate follow-up sequences, track the success of marketing campaigns, and personalize your communication with prospects based on their interaction history. For wildlife removal and pest control businesses, using CRM data to streamline communications can improve customer retention and help you identify patterns in service demand.

How These Pieces Work Together

All of the components of a digital marketing system work in synergy to attract, engage, and convert your audience. Your website serves as the hub of this system, with other components driving traffic to it.

When you publish SEO-optimized content on your website, it improves your search engine ranking, making your business more visible to people searching for pest control services. This content can be shared on your social media platforms, attracting more visitors to your website.

Simultaneously, your online advertising efforts can direct people to your website or a specific landing page to capture leads. These leads can then be nurtured through your email marketing efforts, sending them helpful information and offers that encourage them to avail your services.

Your analytics and reporting tools allow you to monitor the performance of all these components. You can see which tactics are driving the most traffic, which are most successful at converting leads, and where there might be room for improvement. This information allows you to refine your strategy, ensuring your digital marketing system is always evolving and improving.

PART 2
CREATING YOUR SYSTEM

CHAPTER 3
Building an Action Plan

Building a digital marketing action plan is about designing a roadmap towards achieving your business objectives. It involves setting clear goals, understanding your target audience, crafting a compelling value proposition, and mapping out the strategies and tactics you'll employ to reach those goals. To create a successful action plan, you need to integrate the key elements of a digital marketing system discussed in the previous chapter.

Crafting a Digital Marketing Action Plan

Here is a step-by-step guide to creating a digital marketing action plan for your wildlife removal and pest control company:

1. **Set Clear Objectives:** Start by identifying what you want to achieve with your digital marketing efforts. This could be increasing brand awareness, generating more leads, boosting conversions, improving customer retention, or a combination of these.

2. **Define Your Target Audience:** Who are your customers? What are their primary concerns when it comes to pest control or wildlife removal? Understanding your audience's needs, preferences, and behavior will help you tailor your marketing efforts for maximum impact.
3. **Develop Your Value Proposition:** This is a statement that clearly explains what makes your company unique, why customers should choose your services over the competition. It should speak directly to the needs of your target audience and provide compelling reasons for them to choose your company.
4. **Create a Content Strategy:** Plan the kind of content you will create to engage your audience, establish your authority, and improve your SEO ranking. This might include blog posts, how-to guides, infographics, or videos about pest control and wildlife removal.
5. **Outline Your SEO Strategy:** Based on your understanding of your target audience and their search behavior, identify the keywords you will target in your content. Plan how you will build high-quality backlinks and ensure your website's technical performance meets SEO standards.
6. **Plan Your Social Media Activities:** Decide which platforms you will use and what type of content you will share. Create a schedule for regular updates and interaction with your followers.
7. **Develop an Email Marketing Strategy:** Decide how you will capture email leads (for example, through a newsletter sign-up on your website), and plan the kind of content you will send your subscribers. This could include company updates, useful tips, or special offers.

8. **Set up Your Online Advertising Campaigns:** Determine where you will advertise (such as Google Ads or social media platforms), and what kind of ads you will run. Make sure to target your ads to your specific audience and geographic area.
9. **Implement Analytics and Reporting:** Set up tools like Google Analytics to track the performance of your website and marketing activities. Determine the key performance indicators (KPIs) you will monitor, such as website traffic, lead generation, conversion rates, and customer retention.

Putting Your Plan into Action

Once you've created your action plan, it's time to put it into action. This requires consistent execution, regular monitoring, and ongoing adjustment.

As you implement your plan, regularly check your analytics to assess how well your strategies and tactics are working. Don't be afraid to make adjustments along the way – a successful digital marketing strategy is always evolving.

Remember that building a robust digital presence takes time. It's about planting seeds, nurturing them, and patiently waiting for them to bear fruit. With careful planning, diligent execution, and continual optimization, your wildlife removal and pest control company can thrive in the digital landscape.

CHAPTER 4

Understanding Your Target Audience

Identifying the right target audience is a critical step in any digital marketing strategy for pest control and wildlife removal companies. Effectively tailoring your marketing efforts toward your target audience can maximize the return on your marketing investment.

It's essential to conduct thorough market research to gain insights into your potential customers. This includes understanding their demographics, geographic location, behaviors, and preferences. For example, you may find that your target audience consists of homeowners in suburban areas who are concerned about wildlife invading their properties or businesses in urban areas that require pest control services to maintain a clean and safe environment.

Consider the specific needs and pain points of your target audience. What motivates them to seek wildlife removal or pest control services? Are they looking for immediate solutions to an infestation, or do they require long-term preventative measures? Understanding their motivations and pain points will allow you to create marketing messages that resonate with them and address their concerns effectively.

You should also consider the digital channels where your target audience is most active. Are they more likely to search for services on search engines like Google, or do they spend a significant amount of time on social media platforms like Facebook or Instagram? Identifying the channels where your target audience is most engaged will help you allocate your marketing budget and efforts more strategically.

Identifying your target audience is a crucial step in developing a successful digital marketing strategy for pest control and wildlife removal companies. Conducting market research, understanding your audience's demographics, behaviors, preferences, and motivations, as well as identifying the digital channels they frequent, will allow you to tailor your marketing efforts to reach and engage with your ideal customers effectively. By understanding and catering to your target audience, you can optimize your marketing efforts and drive meaningful results for your business.

Incidental vs Non-Incidental Marketing - A Crucial Target Audience Consideration

It is important to understand the distinction between incidental services and non-incidental services for wildlife removal & pest control companies. Incidental services are those that are typically tied to a specific incident or immediate need, such as the removal of a wildlife animal that has entered a property. In such cases, customers are likely to turn to a Google search as their first touchpoint when seeking a solution, making SEO and Paid Search crucial for visibility and attracting potential customers.

On the other hand, non-incidental services are those that are not necessarily tied to an immediate need, such as monthly/quarterly pest control, trap maintenance, or regular inspections. For such services, social media can be a valuable advertising channel as it allows wildlife removal & pest control companies to reach a wider audience of potential customers. These customers may not have an immediate need for the services, but social media advertising can create brand awareness and keep the company top of mind for when a need arises in the future.

Social media ads can also be an effective and cost-efficient way to build brand awareness, particularly for businesses that value brand recognition and not just direct response marketing. Compared to traditional out-of-home marketing or television ads, social media ads can provide a higher reach and exposure to the local market at a lower cost, acting as digital billboards that showcase the brand name and messaging to potential customers.

Customer Journey Mapping

In marketing, understanding the **customer journey** is crucial for creating strategies that resonate with potential customers at each stage of their decision-making process. A typical customer journey can be broken down into five main stages: **Awareness, Consideration, Decision, Retention,** and **Loyalty**. Each stage presents different opportunities to engage with customers, and in the pest control and wildlife removal industry, the right marketing channels and strategies can help move potential customers through this journey seamlessly.

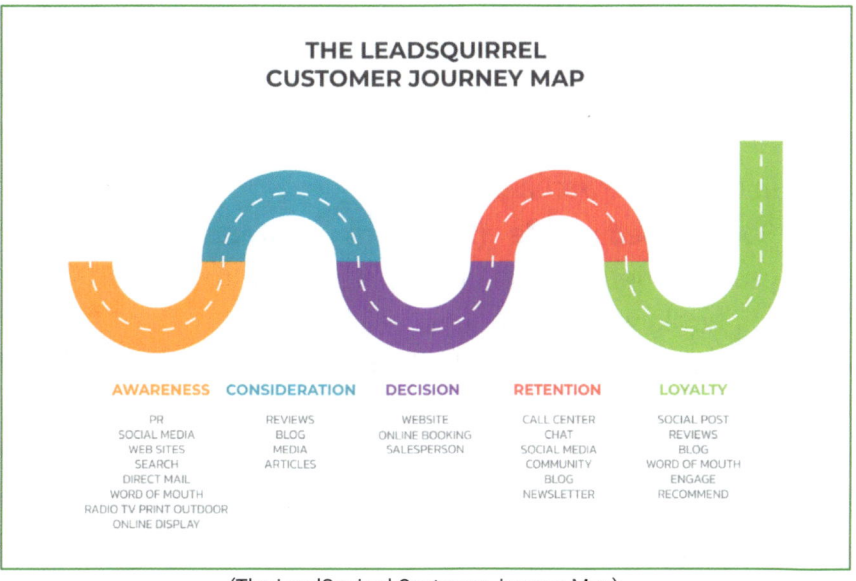

THE LEADSQUIRREL CUSTOMER JOURNEY MAP

AWARENESS	CONSIDERATION	DECISION	RETENTION	LOYALTY
PR SOCIAL MEDIA WEB SITES SEARCH DIRECT MAIL WORD OF MOUTH RADIO TV PRINT OUTDOOR ONLINE DISPLAY	REVIEWS BLOG MEDIA ARTICLES	WEBSITE ONLINE BOOKING SALESPERSON	CALL CENTER CHAT SOCIAL MEDIA COMMUNITY BLOG NEWSLETTER	SOCIAL POST REVIEWS BLOG WORD OF MOUTH ENGAGE RECOMMEND

(The LeadSquirrel Customer Journey Map)

1. Awareness Stage

What Happens Here:

The customer realizes they have a problem that needs solving, whether it's a pest infestation or a wildlife issue. At this stage, they may not know what type of service they need or which company to contact. Their goal is to find out more information about their problem and potential solutions.

Key Marketing Channels:

- **Paid Search (Google Ads):** Targeted ads can capture potential customers at the moment they search for urgent

services like "wildlife removal near me" or "pest control for ants." Paid ads are ideal for getting your business in front of customers quickly and generating awareness.
- **Organic Search (SEO):** High-ranking blog posts, service pages, and optimized website content can attract organic traffic from users searching for wildlife or pest control information. Content like "How to Identify a Raccoon Problem" or "Signs of Termite Damage" can engage users in the early awareness stage.
- **Social Media Ads (Facebook, Instagram):** Sponsored posts targeting local customers can introduce your brand to people who may not yet realize they need your services but could be in the market soon.

Content Focus:

- Blog articles like "How to Tell If You Have Squirrels in Your Attic" or "Common Signs of a Termite Infestation."
- Paid ads targeting search terms like "wildlife removal services" or "pest control near me."
- Educational social media posts and ads offering advice on spotting common pests.

2. Consideration Stage

What Happens Here:

At this stage, the customer has identified their problem and is exploring options to solve it. They might compare different service providers, read reviews, and research pricing and service offerings. Their goal is to gather enough information to make an informed decision.

Key Marketing Channels:

- **Google Business Profile (GBP):** A well-optimized Google Business Profile with positive reviews, up-to-date information, and service details makes it easy for customers to evaluate your business.
- **Content Marketing (Blog Posts, FAQs):** Content like case studies, service comparisons, and in-depth guides can help position your company as an expert. For example, an FAQ page addressing common concerns about wildlife removal techniques or pest control safety can be useful.
- **Social Proof (Reviews and Testimonials):** Platforms like Google, Yelp, and Facebook are critical at this stage. Encourage happy customers to leave reviews and share their experiences. Prospective customers will often look at reviews before making their decision.

Content Focus:

- Comparison guides, such as "How Professional Wildlife Removal Compares to DIY."
- Customer testimonials and case studies highlighting successful outcomes.
- FAQs addressing concerns like pricing, safety, and treatment methods.

3. Decision Stage

What Happens Here:

The customer is ready to choose a service provider. They may have shortlisted a few companies and are now focused on final details like pricing, availability, and ease of communication. The goal is to select a trusted, reliable company that can solve their problem efficiently.

Key Marketing Channels:

- **Paid Search (PPC):** Remarketing ads can target users who have previously visited your website but haven't booked a service yet, encouraging them to come back and complete the action.
- **Email Marketing:** Target customers who have filled out forms or made inquiries but haven't booked yet with follow-up emails, offering additional incentives like discounts or urgent appointments.
- **Website Optimization (Clear Calls to Action):** Ensure your website offers easy-to-find calls to action such as "Schedule an Inspection" or "Get a Free Estimate." The booking process should be simple and streamlined to prevent drop-offs.

Content Focus:

- Strong calls-to-action throughout your website like "Book Now" or "Call Us Today for a Free Estimate."
- Emails or PPC ads offering limited-time deals to encourage action.
- Service-specific landing pages with detailed pricing and service descriptions.

4. Retention Stage

What Happens Here:

The customer has made their choice and used your service, but the journey doesn't end here. Retaining customers is just as important as acquiring new ones. The goal at this stage is to ensure a positive experience so the customer continues using your services for future needs, such as seasonal pest control or wildlife exclusion.

Key Marketing Channels:

- **Email Marketing:** Post-service follow-up emails asking about their experience, providing tips on prevention, and offering reminders for future services (e.g., seasonal pest treatments).
- **Social Media:** Continue engaging customers by offering helpful tips on keeping pests away, sharing updates, and reminding them about your services.
- **Reputation Management (Reviews):** Ask satisfied customers to leave positive reviews. Respond promptly to any negative feedback to show your commitment to customer satisfaction.

Content Focus:

- Educational emails like "How to Keep Your Home Pest-Free After Treatment" or "Seasonal Tips for Preventing Wildlife Intrusion."
- Social media content reminding customers of upcoming seasonal services.
- Prompts for customer reviews to encourage repeat business.

5. Loyalty Stage

What Happens Here:

A loyal customer will return for repeat services and may refer your business to friends or family. The goal here is to create strong brand loyalty, ensuring repeat business and turning your customers into advocates.

Key Marketing Channels:

- **Loyalty Programs/Referral Programs:** Offer discounts or incentives to repeat customers and encourage them to refer friends. This can be promoted through email campaigns, social media, or even in-person at the time of service.
- **Email Marketing (Newsletters):** Send periodic updates about new services, promotions, or helpful tips to stay top-of-mind with your customers.
- **Social Media Engagement:** Encourage customers to share their positive experiences on social media. Run campaigns like "Refer a Friend" where both the referrer and referee get a discount.

Content Focus:

- Emails announcing exclusive offers for loyal customers or referral discounts.
- Social media posts featuring long-time customers or case studies.
- Customer appreciation posts, shout-outs, or giveaways to keep engagement high.

Tying the Customer Journey to Marketing Channels

1. **Awareness Stage**: Use **Paid Search, Organic Search, and Social Media Ads** to introduce your brand and educate potential customers about their problems.
2. **Consideration Stage**: Focus on **Google Business Profile, Content Marketing, and Social Proof** to build trust and provide valuable information to help customers choose your service.
3. **Decision Stage**: Use **PPC Remarketing, Email Marketing**, and an optimized **website** to encourage conversions and make it easy for customers to take the next step.
4. **Retention Stage**: **Email Marketing, Social Media**, and **Reputation Management** help keep customers engaged and ensure they return for future services.
5. **Loyalty Stage**: Build loyalty through **Referral Programs, Newsletters**, and **Social Media Engagement**, encouraging repeat business and referrals.

PART 3

TECHNICAL, TACTICAL EXECUTION

CHAPTER 5
Building an Effective Website

In today's digital age, having a professional website is crucial for wildlife removal and pest control companies. A well-designed and functional website serves as the online face of your business, providing a virtual storefront that is accessible 24/7 to potential customers. It not only enhances your online presence but also establishes credibility and trust with your target audience.

In this chapter, we'll cover:

- The importance of a strong website
- Website Best Practices
- Key Design Elements
- The importance of SEO optimization
- How to build your website

A professional online presence allows you to showcase your services and expertise. It provides a platform to highlight your company's capabilities, qualifications, and experience in wildlife removal and pest control, helping to establish your business as a trusted authority in the industry. This can differentiate you from competitors while showcasing your team, certifications, testimonials, and case studies to build trust with potential customers.

An accessible online platform makes it easy for customers to find and contact you. With a user-friendly design, potential clients can quickly navigate through your services, service areas, contact details, and request quotes or appointments. This ensures your business meets the needs and expectations of today's tech-savvy consumers with a professional and efficient online presence.

Your website can also function as a powerful marketing tool. By leveraging search engine optimization (SEO) and other digital marketing strategies, it can rank higher in search results, attracting targeted traffic. This increased visibility boosts brand exposure, ultimately leading to more leads and customers.

Incorporating a professional website into your digital marketing strategy is essential for wildlife removal and pest control companies. Acting as a virtual storefront, it not only showcases your services and establishes credibility but also provides convenience to potential customers. A well-designed, functional site is a valuable asset, helping your business stand out in a competitive market and driving growth.

Website Best Practices

Before we take a look at some key website design elements, let's talk about some best practices.

CUSTOMER ATTRACTANT

First and foremost, when you build your website, you should put yourself in your potential customer's shoes. Don't just provide info. Ask yourself: "What would I need to see to make a decision on a pest or wildlife company?" These answers will guide many of your best practices.

Your customer will need to see

- Proof that you exist, in the form of Team photos, a company bio, and relevant regional photos
- Proof that you do good work - Show off those reviews!
- Proof that you understand AND have a solution to their problem
- Options to contact you, readily available

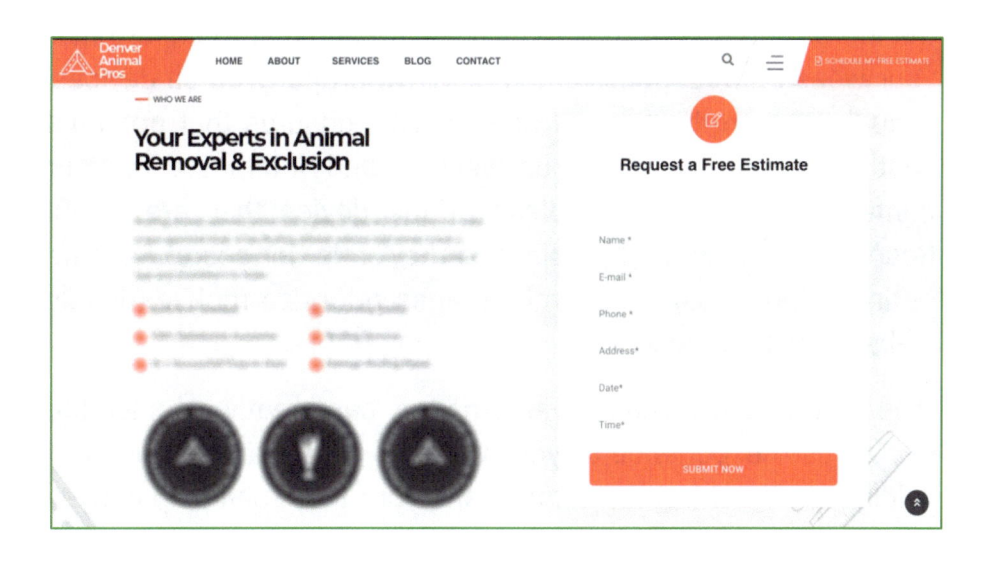

Designing a professional website for wildlife removal and pest control companies requires careful consideration of best practices to ensure an effective online presence. A well-designed website not only attracts potential customers but also provides a seamless user experience, conveys your brand message, and encourages conversions. Here are some key web design best practices that are essential for a professional website in the wildlife removal and pest control industry.

Simplicity and ease of use should be the guiding principles for web design. A clutter-free and intuitive layout with clear navigation is crucial to ensure that visitors can easily find the information they need. This includes a prominently displayed contact information, service areas, and a clear call-to-action (CTA) for requesting quotes or appointments. Keeping the design simple and focused on the core content and functionality helps to create a professional and user-friendly website.

Responsive design is essential for a professional website. With the increasing use of mobile devices, it is crucial to ensure that your website is responsive and displays properly on all devices, including smartphones and tablets. This ensures that potential customers can access your website and interact with your content seamlessly, regardless of the device they are using. Responsive design also plays a key role in search engine optimization (SEO), as search engines prioritize mobile-friendly websites in their rankings.

Visually appealing and relevant imagery can greatly enhance the overall user experience of your website. High-quality images of wildlife, pest control techniques, and your team can help convey your expertise and professionalism. It is important to use images that are relevant to your industry and resonate with your target audience. Additionally, incorporating your branding elements, such as your logo, color scheme, and fonts, throughout the website helps to create a consistent and cohesive brand image.

Conversion Rate Optimization (CRO)

Conversion Rate Optimization (CRO) involves improving your website and landing pages to increase the percentage of visitors who take a desired action, such as booking a service or requesting a quote. Simple strategies like A/B testing different headlines, experimenting with form placements, and using clear, compelling Calls-to-Action (CTAs) can make a significant difference. For wildlife removal companies, ensuring that contact forms are easily accessible, mobile-friendly, and offer instant booking options can significantly increase conversion rates. Regularly testing and refining these elements is key to maximizing the effectiveness of your website.

Optimizing Your Website for Search Engines

Search engine optimization (SEO) is vital for wildlife removal and pest control companies to improve their website's online visibility, attract organic traffic, and generate leads. Best practices for SEO optimization include conducting keyword research to identify relevant keywords and strategically incorporating them into website elements such as title tags, meta descriptions, headers, URLs, and content. Creating high-quality and informative content, optimizing technical elements like website loading speed and mobile-friendliness, and monitoring website performance through analytics tools are also essential for effective SEO optimization.

Having a professional website that follows these SEO best practices is crucial for establishing expertise and authority in the industry, attracting the target audience, and driving more leads. Properly optimized content helps search engines understand the website's relevance, while a user-friendly URL structure and technical optimization ensure smooth crawling and indexing by search engines.

In our next chapter, we'll cover in detail how to implement these SEO strategies.

How to Build Your Website

Building your website might seem like a daunting task. A lot goes into building an effective website, but if you follow these steps, you can create a functional website that will help land new clients day in and day out. This walkthrough will help you build a site without cutting important corners.

Step 1: Define Your Website's Purpose and Goals Before you start building your website, it's important to define its purpose and goals. What do you want your website to achieve? Are you looking to generate leads, provide information about your services, or sell products? Understanding your website's purpose and goals will help you make informed decisions throughout the website building process.

For most wildlife and pest control companies, your goal is lead generation. Keep this in mind when you build your site. You will want your site to be as easy to use as possible. You'll also want to ensure that your site makes it easy to get in touch with your company. When you choose a web page builder, look for samples or templates that have contact forms and click-to-call buttons built in.

Step 2: Choose a Web Page Builder Next, you'll need to choose a web page builder that suits your needs. There are several popular web page builders available that offer easy-to-use drag-and-drop interfaces, making it simple to create a professional-looking website without any coding knowledge. Some popular web page builders include Wix, Squarespace, and WordPress. These platforms offer a wide range of templates and customization options, allowing you to create a unique website that represents your pest control or wildlife removal business.

Step 3: Select a Website Host After choosing a web page builder, you'll need to select a website host. A website host is a service that stores your website's files and makes them accessible to visitors on the internet. Many web page builders, such as Wix and Squarespace, offer built-in hosting services as part of their plans. Alternatively, you can also choose to use a separate website host, such as Bluehost or SiteGround, and connect it to your web page builder.

Step 4: Choose a Domain Name Your domain name is the web address that visitors will use to access your website (e.g., www.yourbusinessname.com). It's important to choose a domain name that is relevant to your pest control or wildlife removal business and easy for visitors to remember. Many web page builders and website hosts offer domain registration services, allowing you to purchase a domain name directly through them.

Step 5: Design Your Website Once you've chosen a web page builder, website host, and domain name, it's time to design your website. Most web page builders offer a wide range of templates that you can customize to suit your business's branding and style. When designing your website, consider the following best practices:

- Use a clean and professional design that reflects your business's image.
- Keep the layout simple and easy to navigate.
- Use high-quality images and graphics that are relevant to your services.
- Include clear and concise content that highlights your services and benefits.
- Ensure that your website is mobile-friendly, as many visitors will access it from mobile devices.

Step 6: Add Essential Pages and Content Your pest control or wildlife removal website should include several essential pages and content to provide a comprehensive overview of your business. These may include:

- Homepage: This is the main page of your website and should provide a clear overview of your business and its services. Include a compelling headline, a brief description of your services, and clear call-to-action buttons.
- Services/Products Page: Create a dedicated page that outlines the pest control or wildlife removal services or products you offer. Include detailed descriptions, pricing, and any special offers.
- About Us Page: This page should provide information about your business, including its history, mission, and team members. Adding personal touches, such as photos and bios, can help establish trust with potential customers.
- Contact Us Page: Make it easy for visitors to contact you by including a dedicated contact page with a contact form, phone number, and email address. You can also include a map with your business location.

- Testimonials/Reviews Page: Highlight positive reviews and testimonials from satisfied customers to build trust and credibility. Include customer quotes, ratings, and reviews to showcase the quality of your services.

Step 7: Optimize for SEO Search engine optimization (SEO) is crucial for ensuring your website appears in search engine results when potential customers search for pest control or wildlife removal services. Include relevant keywords in your website's content, meta tags, and headings to optimize your website for search engines. Make sure your website loads quickly, has descriptive URLs, and includes alt text for images to improve its search engine rankings.

Step 8: Add Additional Features Consider adding additional features to your website to enhance its functionality and user experience. For example, you could include an online booking system that allows customers to schedule appointments directly from your website. You could also integrate social media feeds, a blog, or a newsletter signup to keep visitors engaged and informed about your business.

Step 9: Test and Review Your Website Before launching your website, thoroughly test it to ensure it works well on different devices and browsers. Check for broken links, typos, and other errors. Review your website from a user's perspective and make any necessary improvements to enhance its usability and functionality.

Step 10: Publish and Promote Your Website Once you're satisfied with your website, it's time to publish it and make it live. Connect your domain name to your website host and hit the publish button. After your website is live, promote it through various channels, such as social media, email marketing, and online advertising, to drive traffic and generate leads.

Step 11: Update and Maintain Your Website Regularly update and maintain your website to ensure it stays current, relevant, and secure. Update your content, images, and promotions regularly to keep your website fresh and engaging. Regularly check for security updates and backups to protect your website from potential threats.

Chatbots & Automation

Adding chatbots or automated messaging systems to your website can provide quick, real-time responses to common inquiries, especially for urgent wildlife removal needs. Chatbots can answer frequently asked questions, schedule appointments, and even provide cost estimates, freeing up your team's time to focus on fieldwork. Automation also allows you to maintain customer engagement after hours, ensuring potential clients don't have to wait to get the information they need. When combined with a CRM system, chatbots can also help nurture leads by sending follow-up messages or reminders.

CUSTOMER ATTRACTANT

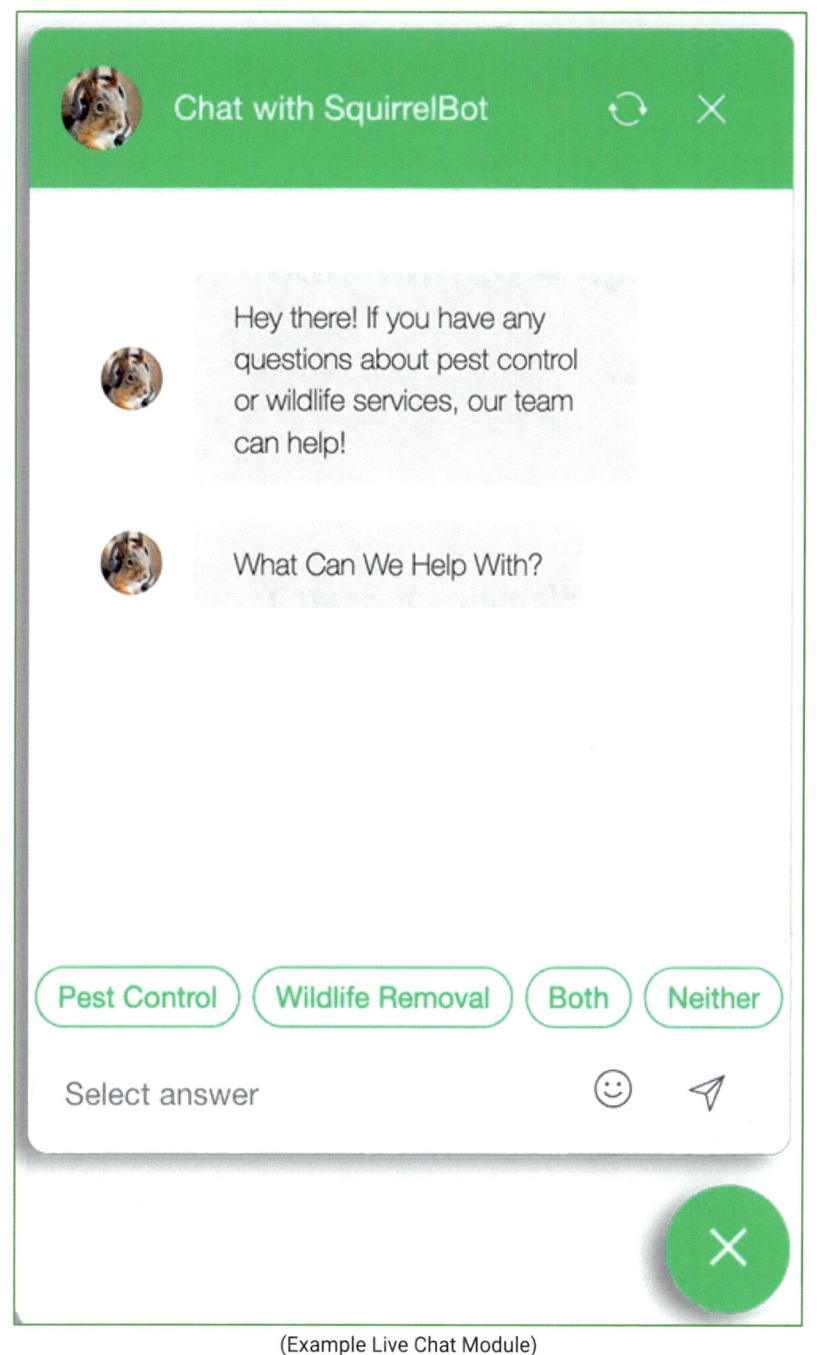

Chat with SquirrelBot

Hey there! If you have any questions about pest control or wildlife services, our team can help!

What Can We Help With?

(Pest Control) (Wildlife Removal) (Both) (Neither)

Select answer

(Example Live Chat Module)

TATE MORGAN

CHAPTER 6
Search Engine Optimization (SEO)

Optimizing Your Website for Search

Search Engine Optimization, often shortened to SEO, is the practice of making changes to your website that improve your odds of showing up in search engines.

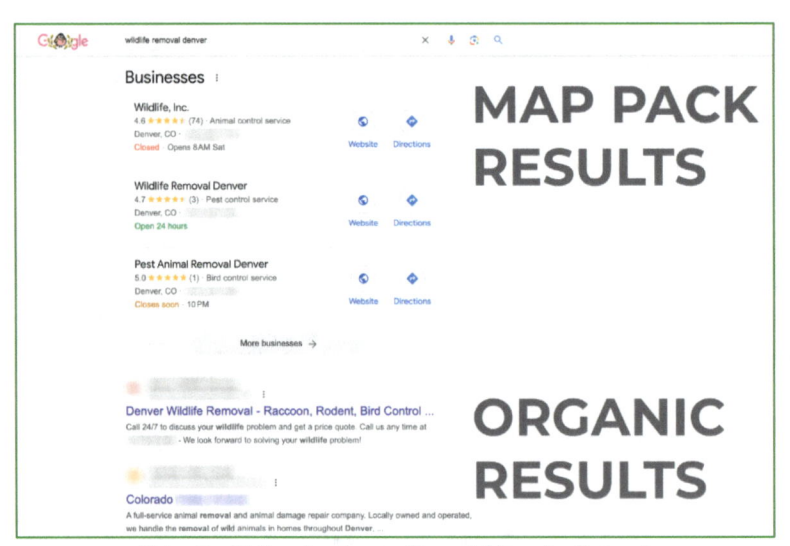

("Map Pack" Results, Top vs. "Organic" Results, Bottom)

CUSTOMER ATTRACTANT

An optimized website can significantly improve your online visibility, attract more organic traffic, and generate leads. To ensure your website ranks highly in search engine results and reaches your target audience effectively, it's essential to follow best practices for SEO optimization.

One of the foundational elements of SEO is keyword research. Identifying the right keywords and incorporating them strategically throughout your website can help search engines understand what your website is about and improve its ranking. This includes optimizing your website's title tags, meta descriptions, headers, URLs, and content with relevant keywords related to wildlife removal, pest control, and your service areas.

Here are some tips for conducting SEO keyword research:

1. Understand your audience: Before you start researching keywords, it's essential to understand who your target audience is and what they're looking for. Use tools like Google Analytics and social media insights to gather information about your audience's demographics, interests, and online behaviors.
2. Brainstorm seed keywords: Create a list of seed keywords that are relevant to your wildlife removal and pest control business. These keywords should reflect the services you offer, the types of pests and animals you handle, and the geographic locations you serve.

You can use a tool like Toptal's Merge Words to combine types of keywords. For example, you could list out all of your covered pests in one column and all of the cities you service in a second column. The resulting merged words list will quickly give you all of your services in all of your cities. This is a great way to get a complete list of your target keywords. This tool is here: https://www.toptal.com/marketing/mergewords 3. Use keyword research tools: There are several keyword research tools available online, including Google Keyword Planner, Ahrefs, and SEMrush. Use these tools to generate keyword ideas, identify search volume, and analyze the competition. 4. Analyze the competition: Analyzing your competitors' websites can help you identify the keywords they're targeting and the strategies they're using to rank higher in search results. Look for gaps in their content and areas where you can differentiate yourself. 5. Focus on long-tail keywords: Long-tail keywords are longer, more specific phrases that are less competitive than short-tail keywords. Use long-tail keywords to target specific niches and increase the chances of ranking higher in search results. 6. Use location-based keywords: If your wildlife removal and pest control business operates in a specific geographic location, use location-based keywords to target local customers. This will help you rank higher in local search results and attract more relevant traffic to your website. 7. Prioritize user intent: When researching keywords, it's essential to prioritize user intent over search volume. Focus on keywords that reflect the searcher's intent and provide solutions to their problems. 8. Monitor and adjust: SEO keyword research is an ongoing process that requires monitoring and adjustment. Monitor your website's search engine rankings and adjust your keyword strategy as needed to improve your results.

Creating high-quality and relevant content is also crucial for SEO optimization. Publishing informative and engaging content that addresses the needs and concerns of your target audience establishes your expertise and authority in the industry. This can include blog posts, articles, infographics, videos, and other types of content that provide value to your visitors. It's important to optimize your content with keywords, use descriptive headings, and incorporate internal and external links to improve its SEO performance.

You can use tools like Adobe Express and Descript to quickly make graphics and videos, while AI Tools like Notion AI and ChatGPT can help you write helpful content. Keep in mind that while AI tools are helpful, they rarely have the industry expertise needed to completely write truly helpful content. You'll still need to edit, rewrite, and provide information yourself. These are helpful tools, not cheat codes!

In addition, optimizing your website's technical elements is essential for SEO success. This includes ensuring that your website loads quickly, is mobile-friendly, and has a user-friendly URL structure. Properly formatting your website's images, using descriptive alt tags, and creating an XML sitemap can also help search engines crawl and index your website more effectively. Regularly monitoring and optimizing your website's performance through analytics tools can provide insights on areas for improvement and help you make data-driven decisions to enhance your website's SEO performance.

Here's an on-page SEO checklist for pest and wildlife removal companies:

1. Keyword Research: Identify relevant keywords that your target audience may use to search for pest control or wildlife removal services. Use tools like Google Keyword Planner or SEMrush to find keywords with high search volume and low competition.

2. Title Tags: This tag controls how your page is titled in search engine search results. Ensure each page on your website has a unique and descriptive title tag that includes your targeted keywords. Keep it under 60 characters and make it compelling to attract clicks in search results.
3. Meta Descriptions: Write unique meta descriptions for each page that summarize the content and include your keywords. Keep it under 155 characters and make it engaging to encourage users to click through to your website.
4. URL Structure: Create SEO-friendly URLs that are descriptive and include your keywords. Avoid using generic URLs with numbers or random characters. For example: www.yourwebsite.com/pest-control-services.
5. Heading Tags: Use heading tags (H1, H2, H3, etc.) to structure your content and make it easy for search engines to understand. Include your keywords in headings to optimize for SEO.
6. Content Optimization: Create high-quality, relevant, and informative content for each page on your website. Use your keywords naturally in the content, but avoid keyword stuffing (placing numerous keywords on a page without purpose or relevance). Aim for a minimum of 300-500 words per page.
7. Image Optimization: Optimize your images by using descriptive file names and alt text that includes your keywords. This helps search engines understand the content of your images and improves accessibility for visually impaired users.
8. Internal Linking: Create internal links within your website to connect related pages. This helps search engines understand the structure and hierarchy of your website, and encourages users to explore more of your content.

9. **Mobile-Friendly Design:** Ensure your website is responsive and mobile-friendly, as a majority of users now access websites on mobile devices. Google also prioritizes mobile-friendly websites in search results.
10. **Site Speed:** Optimize your website for fast loading times as slow websites can negatively impact user experience and SEO rankings. Use tools like Google PageSpeed Insights to identify and fix any speed issues.
11. **Schema Markup:** Implement schema markup, such as LocalBusiness schema, on your website to provide structured data that helps search engines understand your business details, such as name, address, phone number, and reviews.
12. **Social Sharing:** Add social sharing buttons to your website to encourage visitors to share your content on social media, which can help drive more traffic and increase your online visibility.
13. **User Experience:** Ensure your website is easy to navigate, visually appealing, and provides a positive user experience. This includes clear calls-to-action, easy contact forms, and a professional design.
14. **Analytics and Tracking:** Set up Google Analytics and Google Search Console to track your website's performance, monitor traffic, and identify areas for improvement.

Voice Search Optimization

Voice search is becoming increasingly common, especially with the rise of smart speakers like Amazon Alexa and Google Home. Optimizing your website for voice search can help ensure your business appears in voice-driven queries. Focus on natural, conversational phrases, such as "Who can remove bats from my attic?" or "Wildlife control services near me." This requires structuring your content to answer common questions clearly and concisely. Including an FAQ section on your website that addresses common voice search queries can help capture this growing audience, particularly as more consumers rely on voice-activated assistants for local service recommendations.

How to Structure Your Pest Control & Wildlife Removal Website for SEO Success

A well-structured website is the backbone of a successful online presence, particularly for service-oriented businesses like wildlife removal & pest control. Not only does a clear and logical site structure enhance user experience by making it easier for visitors to find the information they need, but it also plays a critical role in search engine optimization (SEO). A well-organized website helps search engines like Google understand the hierarchy and relevance of your content, which can lead to higher rankings in search results.

Additionally, a structured site with strong internal linking can positively impact your Google Business Profile ranking, making your business more visible in local search results. This visibility is essential for attracting potential customers in your service area, driving more traffic to your site, and ultimately converting that traffic into leads. Lets explore the ideal website structure for a wildlife & pest business, using Phoenix, AZ, and surrounding cities as examples, to help you build a site that's both user-friendly and optimized for search engines.

1. Home Page: The Gateway to Your Services

Your home page is the central hub of your website. It should link directly to your main service pages and location-specific pages, offering users and search engines an easy way to navigate your site.

- **Example Title:** Home
- **Example URL:** /

From the home page, users should be able to access all major service categories, such as "Wildlife Removal Services" and "Rodent Removal Services."

2. Main Service Pages: Broad Categories for Easy Navigation

Your main service pages act as the top-level categories for your services. These pages should link to more specific service pages and relevant location pages.

- **Example Title:** Wildlife Removal Services
- **Example URL:** `/wildlife-removal-services/`

These pages should guide users to more specific services like "Squirrel Removal Services" and "Bat Removal Services."

3. Service-Specific Pages: Detailed Information on Each Service

Service-specific pages delve into the details of each service you offer. They should link to location-specific service pages to create a logical flow of information.

- **Example Title:** Squirrel Removal Services
- **Example URL:** `/squirrel-removal-services/`

Each of these pages should provide comprehensive information on the service and link to location-specific pages, such as "Squirrel Removal in Phoenix, AZ."

4. Location-Specific Service Pages: Targeting Local Search Queries

To capture local search traffic, create location-specific pages for each service. These pages should be internally linked from the corresponding service-specific pages and should contain localized content.

- **Example Title:** Squirrel Removal in Phoenix, AZ
- **Example URL:** `/squirrel-removal-phoenix-az/`

Location-specific pages help you rank for local searches like "squirrel removal in Phoenix" or "bat removal in Mesa."

5. Fact/FAQ Pages: Addressing Specific Questions

To further support your SEO strategy, create fact or FAQ pages that answer specific questions about each service in each location. These pages should be linked from the corresponding location-specific service pages.

- **Example Title:** How to Identify Squirrels in Phoenix
- **Example URL:** `/blog/identify-squirrels-phoenix/`

These pages serve as valuable resources for both users and search engines, helping to establish your site as an authoritative source of information.

Ideal Website Structure Table

Here's a table outlining the ideal website structure for a wildlife removal business, with a focus on creating SEO-optimized silos through internal linking:

Page Type	Example Title	Example URL	Internal Linking Strategy
Home Page	Home	/	Link to primary service pages, location pages, and blog categories.
Main Service Page	Wildlife Removal Services	/wildlife-removal-services/	Link to service-specific pages and location pages.
Service-Specific Page	Squirrel Removal Services	/squirrel-removal-services/	Link to related service pages, blog posts answering specific questions, and location pages.
Service-Specific in Location	Squirrel Removal in Phoenix, AZ	/squirrel-removal-phoenix-az/	Link to the main squirrel removal page, location pages, and relevant blog posts.
Location-Specific Page	Wildlife Removal in Phoenix, AZ	/wildlife-removal-phoenix-az/	Link to all service-specific pages related to this location and blog posts about local issues.
Blog Category Page	Wildlife Control Tips	/wildlife-control-tips/	Link to relevant blog posts, service pages, and location pages.
Blog Post - General	How to Identify Squirrel Infestations	/blog/identify-squirrel-infestations/	Link to squirrel removal service page and related blog posts.
Blog Post - Location Specific	How to Deal with Squirrels in Phoenix, AZ	/blog/squirrels-phoenix-az/	Link to squirrel removal service page in Phoenix and other

Page Type	Example Title	Example URL	Internal Linking Strategy
			location-specific posts.
FAQ Page	Frequently Asked Questions about Wildlife Removal	/faqs/	Link to service-specific pages and relevant blog posts.
Contact Page	Contact Us	/contact/	Link to all main service pages, location pages, and the homepage.
About Us Page	About Our Wildlife Removal Services	/about-us/	Link to the home page, main service pages, and contact page.
Testimonials/Reviews Page	Customer Reviews	/customer-reviews/	Link to service-specific pages and the home page.
Service Area Page	Service Areas	/service-areas/	Link to all location-specific pages.
Sitemap	Sitemap	/sitemap/	Link to all pages for easier crawling by search engines.

Example of a Complete Silo Structure

Here's an example of how your site might be structured:

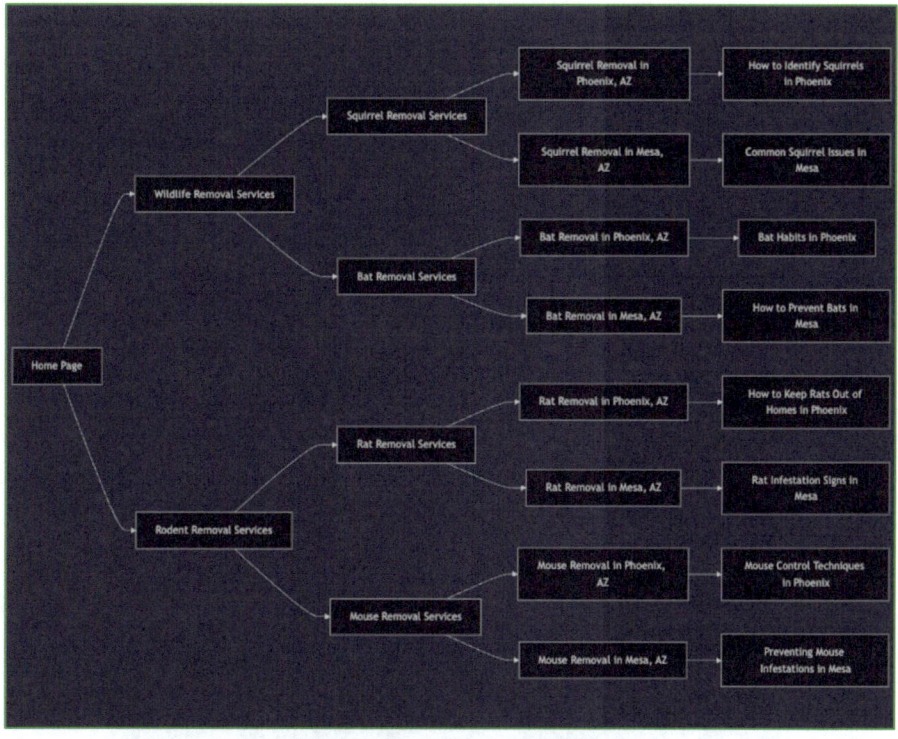

(Example of topical silos for SEO)

By implementing this structured approach, your wildlife removal business in Phoenix, AZ, and surrounding cities will not only provide a better user experience but also improve your rankings in search engine results. The concepts used to build this site structure will apply to both pest & wildlife websites, regardless of location. A well-organized website helps search engines understand the hierarchy and relevance of your content, ultimately driving more traffic to your site.

Local SEO - Google Business Profiles & Other Critical Listings

As a wildlife removal and pest control company, optimizing your online presence for local search is essential to attracting customers in your target area. Local SEO strategies can significantly boost your visibility in local search results, and one of the most impactful ways to do this is through optimizing your **Google Business Profile (GBP)** (formerly Google My Business).

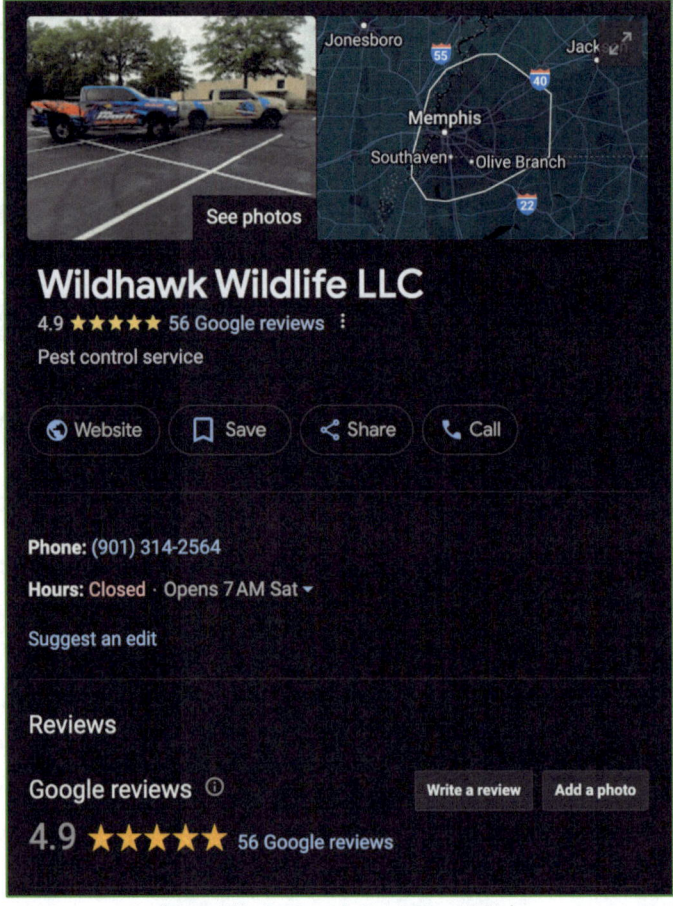

(Example of a Google Business Profile)

Why Google Business Profile Optimization is Key for Wildlife Removal and Pest Control Companies

A well-optimized GBP can substantially enhance your local SEO efforts by making your business more visible in Google Search and Google Maps. This is particularly important in industries like wildlife removal, where customers often need urgent services and are more likely to turn to local search for immediate help. Here's a detailed breakdown of how to optimize your GBP for search:

Step-by-Step Guide to Optimizing Your Google Business Profile

1. Claim and Verify Your Profile

First, make sure your business is claimed and verified on Google Business Profile. Without verification, your business won't have full control over its profile, and inaccurate information could mislead potential customers or hurt your rankings. Ensure the verification process is completed so you can manage and update the profile regularly.

2. Accurate and Complete Business Information

Make sure your GBP contains accurate and comprehensive business details, including:

- **Business Name**: Use your official business name without keyword stuffing (which can hurt rankings).
- **Address and Phone Number**: Double-check that these details are correct and match other online listings.
- **Service Areas**: For wildlife removal and pest control companies, defining service areas is critical. Include all

areas you serve, even those outside your immediate location, as this can help you show up in more localized searches.
- **Business Hours**: Keep your business hours updated, especially during holidays or seasonal changes.
- **Website**: Link directly to your website's homepage or a specific service page to ensure potential customers find relevant information quickly.

3. Select the Right Business Categories

Choosing the appropriate categories for your business is vital to ranking in local searches. Since Google currently does not have a specific "wildlife removal" category (as of August 2024), select **Animal Control Service** as your primary category, as it's the most relevant. Google representatives have suggested that a **Wildlife Removal** category may be added as early as November 2024, so keep an eye on updates and switch to this category when available.

4. Add High-Quality Images and Videos

Visual content plays a significant role in building trust and attracting potential customers. Upload high-resolution images of your team, trucks, and completed jobs to showcase your professionalism. Include before-and-after photos of wildlife removal or pest control work, and even short videos explaining your services or introducing your team.

5. Leverage Google Posts and Q&A

Use the **Posts** feature on GBP to share updates, promotions, or informative content. Regular posts can help you engage with customers and keep your profile active. You can also answer common customer questions through the **Q&A** section, offering helpful insights and further positioning yourself as an expert in the industry.

6. Utilize Messaging Features

Enable **Messaging** to allow potential customers to contact you directly through Google. This real-time communication can be a deciding factor for customers facing urgent pest or wildlife issues. Be sure to respond promptly to inquiries to improve customer experience and increase conversions.

7. Consistent NAP Information Across Listings

Consistency is crucial for local SEO. Ensure that your business's **Name, Address, and Phone number (NAP)** are identical across all online directories, including Yelp, Bing Places, and industry-specific platforms. Inconsistent NAP information can confuse search engines and harm your rankings.

The Importance of Regular Reviews and Customer Engagement

One of the most critical components of a successful GBP optimization strategy is acquiring a steady stream of **new customer reviews**. Not only do reviews help build trust with potential customers, but they also signal to Google that your business is active and reputable, which can significantly boost your local search ranking.

- **Encourage Satisfied Customers to Leave Reviews**: After completing a service, ask satisfied clients to leave a review on your Google Business Profile. A personalized request,

either in person or through follow-up emails or texts, can increase the likelihood of getting reviews.
- **Respond to All Reviews**: Whether the feedback is positive or negative, respond professionally to every review. Positive reviews should be acknowledged with gratitude, while negative reviews should be addressed with a solution-focused approach. Quick and respectful responses show you value customer feedback and can also improve your business reputation.

Regular reviews also create a sense of activity and relevancy around your profile, which search engines consider when determining rankings. Additionally, they provide fresh content for your GBP, which keeps it active and relevant in local searches.

Maintain and Monitor Your GBP Regularly

Optimizing your GBP is not a one-time task. It's crucial to regularly monitor and update your profile to reflect any changes in your business, such as new services, additional service areas, or updated hours. Keep track of how your GBP is performing by reviewing insights available in the platform, including the number of views, clicks, and calls you receive. Use this data to refine your local SEO strategy continually.

Implementing local SEO strategies, such as optimizing your Google Business Profile and maintaining consistent NAP information across online directories, can help you improve your local search rankings, increase your online visibility in your target area, and attract more local customers for your wildlife removal and pest control services. Remember to regularly monitor and update your local SEO efforts to ensure that your online presence remains optimized and effective in attracting local customers.

CHAPTER 7
Pay-Per-Click (PPC) Advertising

Google Ads, formerly known as Google AdWords, is a pay-per-click (PPC) advertising platform that allows businesses to create and run ads that appear on Google search results and other Google platforms. This is one of the most important marketing avenues for pest and wildlife removal companies because a significant number of your potential customers start their hiring journey with an online search.

If you want to show up first in the search results quickly, PPC advertising is the way to make it happen. This speed comes at a cost, though. Rather than paying per lead, you're paying every time someone clicks on your ad. For this reason, it's critical that you are properly targeting your ads and that your potential customers are landing on a website that is easy to navigate and even easier to get in touch.

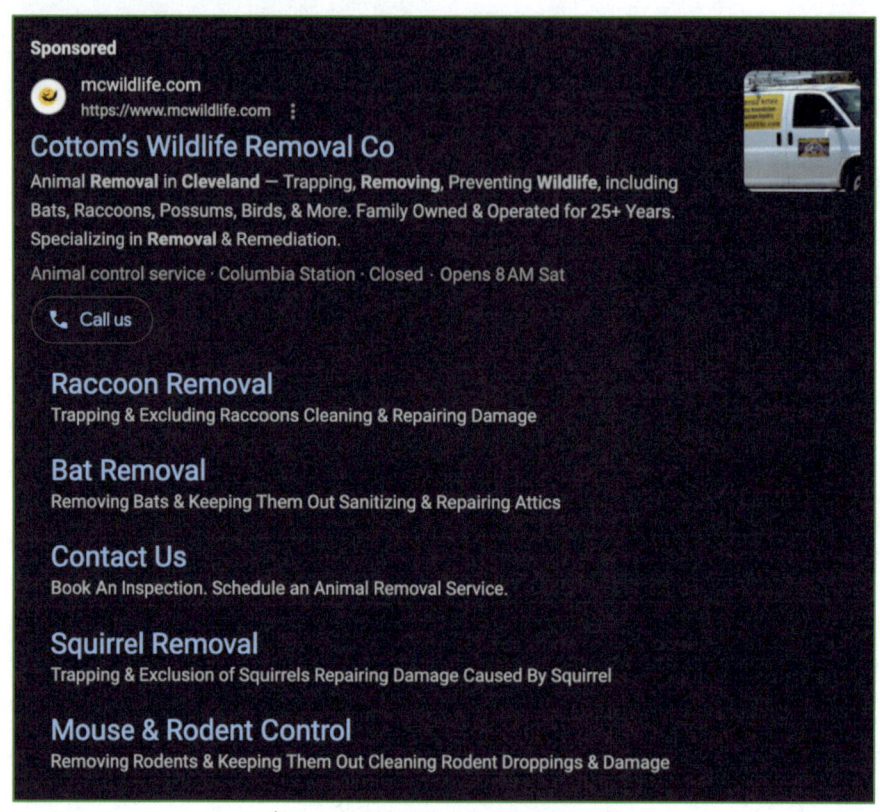

(Example of a strong Google PPC Ad)

One of the key advantages of Google Ads is its ability to target specific keywords and geographic locations. Wildlife removal and pest control companies can target keywords related to their services, such as "wildlife removal services" or "pest control near me," to ensure that their ads are shown to users who are actively searching for these services in their local area. This highly targeted approach can result in more qualified leads and higher conversion rates, as the ads are reaching users who are actively interested in wildlife removal or pest control services.

Google Ads provides businesses with control over their advertising budget and performance. Companies can set a daily budget for their ads, and only pay when users click on their ads, making it a cost-effective advertising option. Additionally, Google Ads provides detailed performance metrics, allowing businesses to track the success of their ads, make data-driven decisions, and optimize their campaigns for better results. This level of control and transparency can help wildlife removal and pest control companies make informed decisions about their advertising strategies and maximize their return on investment (ROI).

Google Ads can be a powerful advertising tool for wildlife removal and pest control companies, offering targeted reach, control over advertising budget, and detailed performance tracking. By leveraging Google Ads effectively, wildlife removal and pest control companies can increase their online visibility, attract more qualified leads, and ultimately grow their business.

Setting Up PPC Ads

When it comes to setting up Google Ads for wildlife removal and pest control companies, it's important to follow best practices to ensure a successful campaign. Here are some key steps to consider:

1. Keyword Research: Conduct thorough keyword research to identify the most relevant and effective keywords for your wildlife removal and pest control services. This includes identifying keywords related to the types of pests you specialize in, the services you offer, and the geographic locations you serve. Use keyword research tools, such as Google Keyword Planner, to identify keywords with high search volume and low competition.

2. Campaign Structure: Create well-structured campaigns and ad groups to ensure that your ads are organized and targeted. Group keywords into relevant ad groups and create specific ads for each ad group. This allows you to customize your ad copy and landing pages for maximum relevance and quality score, which can help improve your ad performance.
3. Ad Creation: Craft compelling and relevant ad copy that highlights the unique selling propositions of your wildlife removal and pest control services. Use ad extensions, such as call extensions or location extensions, to provide additional information and make your ads more prominent. Test multiple ad variations to identify which ones perform best and continually optimize your ad copy to improve your click-through rates (CTR) and conversion rates.
4. Landing Page Optimization: Create landing pages that are tailored to your ads and provide a seamless user experience. Ensure that your landing pages load quickly, have clear and concise messaging, and prominently display your call-to-action (CTA). Include relevant keywords in your landing page content and meta tags for SEO optimization. Regularly monitor and optimize your landing pages for better conversion rates.
5. Budget and Bidding Strategy: Set a budget that aligns with your advertising goals and ensures that you can sustain your campaign over time. Choose an appropriate bidding strategy, such as manual bidding or automated bidding, based on your campaign objectives and budget. Monitor your campaign performance regularly and adjust your bids and budget as needed to maximize your ROI.

6. Tracking and Analysis: Set up conversion tracking to measure the effectiveness of your Google Ads campaign. Use Google Analytics to track the performance of your landing pages and gain insights into user behavior. Analyze your campaign data regularly to identify areas for improvement and make data-driven decisions to optimize your campaign for better results.

By following these best practices, wildlife removal and pest control companies can set up a successful Google Ads campaign that drives targeted traffic, generates qualified leads, and ultimately helps grow their business.

Writing and Creating Ads for PPC Success

One of the most difficult pieces of the PPC puzzle are the ads themselves. How do you write an ad that makes searchers want to click and become customers? Follow the steps below to create ads that are highly likely to turn searchers into customers.

1. Understand Your Target Audience: Before you start writing your ads, it's important to have a clear understanding of your target audience. Consider their needs, pain points, and motivations when crafting your ad copy. This will help you create ads that resonate with your audience and compel them to take action.
2. Use Attention-Grabbing Headlines: The headline is the first thing users see in your ad, so make it compelling and attention-grabbing. Use action words, numbers, and emotional triggers to create a sense of urgency and encourage users to click on your ad.

3. **Highlight Your Unique Selling Proposition (USP)**: What sets your wildlife removal or pest control business apart from the competition? Whether it's your expertise, quick response time, or eco-friendly methods, highlight your USP in your ad copy to differentiate yourself and entice users to choose your services.
4. **Focus on Benefits**: Instead of just listing features, focus on the benefits of your services in your ad copy. How will your wildlife removal or pest control services solve your customers' problems or improve their lives? Clearly communicate the value of your services to your audience.
5. **Use Relevant Keywords**: Incorporate relevant keywords in your ad copy to ensure your ads are targeting the right audience. This will help improve your ad's relevance and quality score, which can result in higher ad rankings and lower costs per click.
6. **Include a Call-to-Action (CTA)**: Your PPC ads should include a clear and compelling call-to-action (CTA) that tells users what you want them to do next. Whether it's "Call Now," "Get a Free Quote," or "Book an Appointment," make sure your CTA is prominent and creates a sense of urgency.
7. **Test Different Ad Variations**: Create multiple ad variations and test them to see which ones perform the best. Experiment with different headlines, ad copy, and CTAs to identify what resonates best with your target audience and drives the highest conversions.
8. **Be Honest and Transparent**: Avoid making exaggerated or false claims in your PPC ads. Be honest and transparent about your services and pricing to build trust with your audience. Misleading ads can result in negative feedback and damage your reputation.

9. Use Ad Extensions: Take advantage of ad extensions, such as call extensions, location extensions, and review extensions, to provide additional information and make your ads more compelling. Ad extensions can help increase your ad's visibility and provide more context to users.
10. Continuously Monitor and Optimize: PPC advertising requires ongoing monitoring and optimization. Regularly review your ad performance, make data-driven decisions, and optimize your ads based on the results. Test different ad elements and make adjustments to improve your ad's performance over time.

Optimizing PPC Campaigns for Maximum ROI

To achieve maximum return on investment (ROI) with your Google Ads campaign, it's important to implement advanced strategies such as utilizing negative keywords and leveraging bid adjustments. Here are some key tips for optimizing your Google Ads campaign for wildlife removal and pest control companies:

1. Negative Keywords: Implementing negative keywords is a powerful strategy to filter out irrelevant searches and ensure that your ads are shown only to highly relevant and qualified users. For example, if you offer wildlife removal services but do not handle bird removal, you can add "bird" as a negative keyword to prevent your ads from appearing for searches related to bird removal. Regularly review and update your negative keyword list to continuously refine your targeting and minimize wasted ad spend on irrelevant searches.

Negative keywords can be a great way to prevent those pesky Animal Control calls. If you're not catching strays, wrangling dogs, and dealing with cats, you'll want to use negative keywords to prevent people who are searching for your local animal warden from seeing and clicking on your ads. 2. Bid Adjustments: Take advantage of bid adjustments to optimize your bids for different factors such as location, device, and time of day. For example, if you find that your ads perform better on mobile devices compared to desktops, you can increase your bid for mobile devices to capture more mobile traffic. Similarly, if you notice that your ads perform better during certain times of the day, you can adjust your bids accordingly. Continuously monitor your campaign performance and use bid adjustments strategically to allocate your budget effectively and maximize your ROI. 3. Ad Extensions: Utilize ad extensions to enhance the visibility and relevance of your ads. Ad extensions, such as call extensions, location extensions, and site link extensions, provide additional information to potential customers and can improve the performance of your ads. For instance, a call extension can allow users to directly call your business from the ad, making it easier for them to contact you. Experiment with different ad extensions and monitor their performance to identify which ones are driving the best results for your campaign.

Local Services Ads - A Must-Have For Pest Control Providers

One of the most effective developments in Google's advertising ecosystem in the last few years is Local Services Ads. These ads are pay-per-lead (instead of PPC), meaning you'll only pay when you have a conversation with a potential customer.

CUSTOMER ATTRACTANT

Unfortunately, these ads are not available for Wildlife Removal providers just yet, but if you've got a Pest Control license and carry insurance that covers pest control services in your state, you can take advantage of these powerful pay-per-lead ads.

Note: Google Reps have suggested that Local Service Ads will be available for Wildlife Removal companies as early as November 2024. Keep an eye out for this update, as it will be a game-changer!

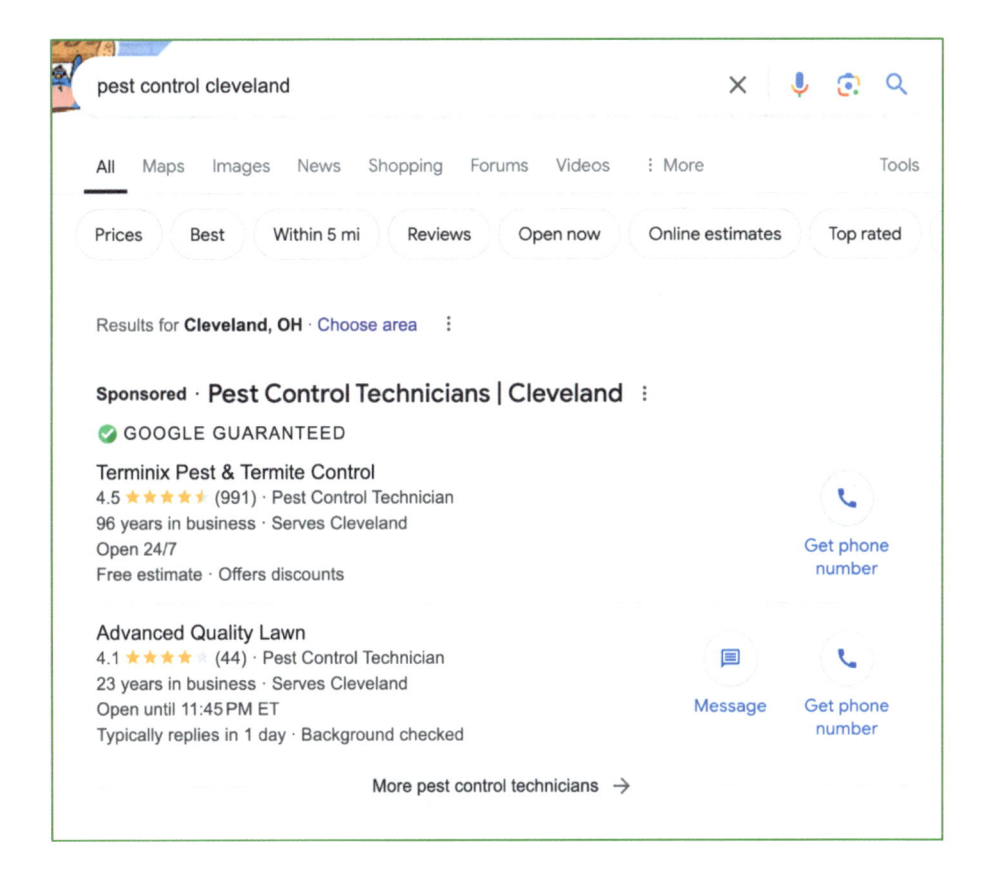

Local services ads prominently display registered businesses at the absolute top of Google's search results any time someone locally searches for a service. In order to be eligible for these ads,

67

you must go through an eligibility check conducted by Google. This check will include

- A confirmation of your state pest control license
- A confirmation of your business Liability Insurance
- Background checks for all customer-facing employees
- Historical information about your business and behavior

Once this check is complete, your Local Service Ad will display your business' name, reviews, phone number, and a green "Google Guaranteed" badge. These ads have proven an incredible tool for lead generation, cutting cost per lead by as much as 60% in some cases.

CHAPTER 8
Social Media Marketing

Leveraging Social Media for Wildlife Removal and Pest Control Companies

Social media is an invaluable tool for wildlife removal and pest control companies, providing an effective way to connect with your audience, build brand awareness, and position yourself as a trusted expert in the industry. Today's consumers look to social platforms not just for entertainment, but also to vet businesses and ensure they are reputable. Regular, thoughtful engagement on social media fosters trust, making it a powerful part of your business strategy.

Why Social Media Matters for Your Business

Potential customers often visit social media profiles to assess whether a company is credible and active. If members of your local community see that you post regularly, engage with followers, and showcase your involvement in local projects, they're more likely to view your business as trustworthy and approachable.

Additionally, many people turn to social platforms like Facebook, Instagram, and Nextdoor to find local service providers. Community-driven groups are frequently used to ask for recommendations, and businesses with a strong presence are more likely to be mentioned in these conversations. By maintaining a consistent and engaging social media presence, you increase your chances of being top-of-mind when someone needs wildlife removal or pest control services.

Key Strategies for Effective Social Media Use

To maximize the impact of your social media presence, it's important to develop a clear and strategic approach. Here are essential tips to guide your efforts:

1. Develop a Strong Content Strategy

A well-defined content strategy is the foundation of an effective social media presence. Your content should be engaging, informative, and aligned with the interests of your target audience. Consider sharing:

- **Educational posts** about wildlife and pest behavior, prevention tips, and seasonal challenges.
- **Success stories and case studies** showcasing the problems you've solved for customers.
- **Team spotlights** that introduce key members of your company to humanize your brand.
- **Visual content** like videos of safe animal removals or before-and-after photos to capture attention.

Consistency is crucial—maintain a regular posting schedule so your audience stays engaged. Posting sporadically may lead to reduced visibility, while consistent updates keep your brand fresh in people's minds.

2. Engage Actively with Your Audience

Engagement is more than just posting content—it's about building relationships. Make an effort to respond promptly to comments, messages, and inquiries. When potential customers see that you're responsive and helpful, it reinforces the idea that you're approachable and reliable. Don't hesitate to:

- **Ask questions** in your posts to encourage interaction.
- **Join community discussions**, whether they occur in comment sections or local groups.
- **Use social media as customer service**, addressing any questions or concerns quickly and professionally.

Engaging with your audience builds a sense of community, making customers more likely to choose your services when the need arises.

3. Share Educational Content

Position yourself as an expert by sharing content that educates your audience. Informational posts about wildlife habits, pest prevention tips, and insights into your removal processes help potential customers understand the value of professional wildlife and pest control services. By offering helpful tips and industry knowledge, you build credibility, encouraging customers to trust your expertise.

- Example topics include "Why Bats are Beneficial (But Not in Your Home)" or "Top 5 Signs You Have a Squirrel Problem."
- Share **seasonal content** as well, such as "Springtime Pest Prevention Tips" to keep your feed relevant throughout the year.

4. Highlight Local Community Involvement

Social media is a great platform for showcasing your company's commitment to the local community. Share posts about events, sponsorships, or volunteer activities that your business supports. For example, post about your team's involvement in community cleanups, educational workshops, or fundraising events. This demonstrates that you're not just a service provider, but a responsible and caring member of the local community.

Local connections matter, and people are more likely to trust companies that they see giving back to the community.

5. Ensure Visual Consistency with Your Branding

Make your social media profiles visually cohesive and representative of your brand. Use high-quality visuals, such as your company logo, photos of your team, and branded graphics, to create a professional and polished appearance. Consistency in your branding—colors, fonts, and logo placement—across all posts and profiles builds recognition and helps you stand out in a crowded market.

Additionally, visually engaging content like **before-and-after photos**, **wildlife videos**, and **behind-the-scenes footage** of your team at work can capture attention and encourage followers to engage with your posts.

6. Monitor Analytics and Adjust Your Strategy

Regularly tracking the performance of your social media efforts is essential for continuous improvement. Use social media analytics tools to monitor key metrics like:

- **Engagement** (likes, comments, shares)
- **Reach** (how many people see your content)
- **Follower growth**
- **Click-through rates** to your website or services.

Analyzing these metrics allows you to see what's working and what's not. For example, you may find that educational videos receive higher engagement than static images, prompting you to shift your content strategy accordingly. Using data-driven insights helps you optimize your social media strategy for better results over time.

The Power of Reviews and Recommendations on Social Media

Another critical aspect of social media success is leveraging **reviews and recommendations**. Social platforms, particularly Facebook and Nextdoor, are hotspots for local service provider recommendations. Encourage satisfied customers to leave reviews on your business's social media profiles and actively ask them to tag or mention your company in local recommendation threads.

Positive social proof not only boosts your credibility but also makes it more likely for your business to be recommended when someone asks, "Can anyone recommend a good wildlife removal service?"

Social Media Advertising - Stay Top of Mind

Leveraging Social Media Advertising for Wildlife Removal and Pest Control Companies

Social media advertising can be a powerful tool for wildlife removal and pest control companies to reach a wider audience, generate leads, and drive business growth. By leveraging the advanced targeting capabilities of platforms like Facebook and Nextdoor, your business can connect with local customers, promote specific services, and boost brand awareness.

Why Facebook and Nextdoor Are Key Platforms for Wildlife and Pest Control Advertising

As of now, **Facebook** continues to dominate the social media advertising space, especially for wildlife removal and pest control businesses. Facebook's vast reach, combined with its detailed targeting options, allows you to fine-tune your audience by location, demographics, interests, and behaviors. You can even retarget individuals who have visited your website but haven't converted into customers yet, or market new offers to your existing client base.

Another strong option for local advertising is **Nextdoor**, a platform specifically designed to foster conversations within neighborhoods. Nextdoor allows you to place ads directly in front of community members by targeting specific neighborhoods or zip codes. This hyper-local approach can be especially effective if you're already servicing a particular neighborhood, as it boosts

CUSTOMER ATTRACTANT

your visibility among nearby potential customers. Keep in mind, however, that Nextdoor tends to have an older user base compared to other social platforms, which may influence your ad creative and messaging.

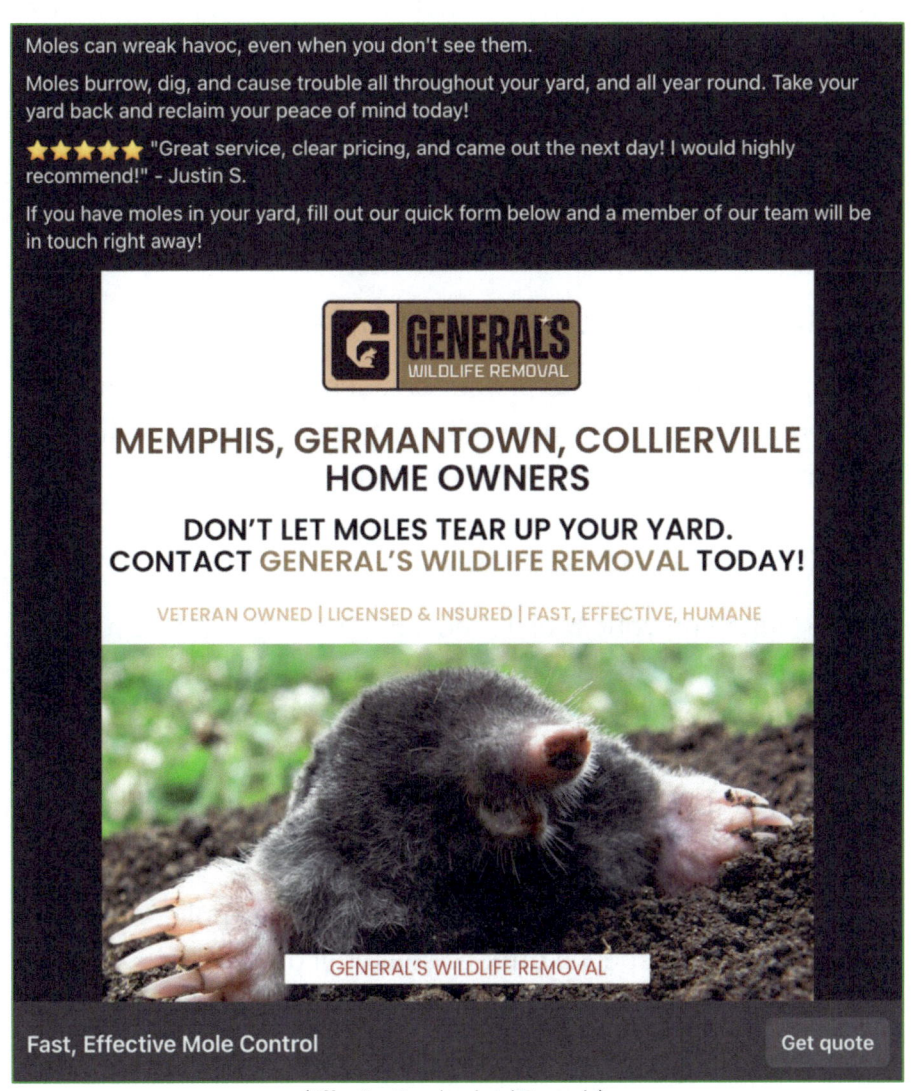

> Moles can wreak havoc, even when you don't see them.
>
> Moles burrow, dig, and cause trouble all throughout your yard, and all year round. Take your yard back and reclaim your peace of mind today!
>
> ★★★★★ "Great service, clear pricing, and came out the next day! I would highly recommend!" - Justin S.
>
> If you have moles in your yard, fill out our quick form below and a member of our team will be in touch right away!
>
> **GENERAL'S WILDLIFE REMOVAL**
>
> **MEMPHIS, GERMANTOWN, COLLIERVILLE HOME OWNERS**
>
> **DON'T LET MOLES TEAR UP YOUR YARD. CONTACT GENERAL'S WILDLIFE REMOVAL TODAY!**
>
> VETERAN OWNED | LICENSED & INSURED | FAST, EFFECTIVE, HUMANE
>
> GENERAL'S WILDLIFE REMOVAL
>
> Fast, Effective Mole Control — Get quote

(Effective Facebook Ad Example)

Understanding the Nature of Social Media Ads

It's important to recognize that social media users aren't typically browsing with the intention of finding a service provider. They're more likely checking in on family members, looking at community updates, or engaging with personal interests. As a result, your ad is an interruption in their feed, which can mean lower conversion rates compared to more direct marketing channels like SEO or PPC. However, this doesn't negate the value of social media advertising—it's still an important tool for building brand awareness and staying top-of-mind for potential customers.

Key Strategies for Effective Social Media Advertising

To maximize the success of your social media ads, it's essential to approach each campaign with a clear strategy and focused objectives. Here are some key tips to guide your efforts:

1. Define Your Objectives Clearly

Before launching your social media advertising campaign, define your primary goals. Are you aiming to increase brand awareness, generate leads, drive website traffic, or promote a specific service? Having clear objectives will help shape the design, targeting, and messaging of your ads, ensuring they align with your broader business goals.

- If your goal is **lead generation**, for example, you might focus on a special offer or seasonal promotion.
- If you're looking to **increase brand awareness**, you might create ads that introduce your business and highlight your services in a more general sense.

2. Leverage Audience Targeting

One of the most significant advantages of social media advertising is the ability to target specific audiences with precision. Both Facebook and Nextdoor offer robust targeting features, allowing you to define your audience based on:

- **Location**: Narrow down to specific neighborhoods or zip codes.
- **Demographics**: Age, gender, education level, and more.
- **Interests and Behaviors**: Focus on users with interests related to home improvement, animal care, or local services. This ensures that your ads are reaching the right people—those most likely to need and engage with your wildlife removal or pest control services.

3. Create Compelling Ad Creatives

Because your ads will interrupt users' social media experience, it's crucial that they stand out and grab attention immediately. High-quality visuals, engaging videos, and concise, compelling copy can make all the difference. Your ad creative should:

- Clearly communicate your **value proposition** (e.g., humane wildlife removal, eco-friendly pest control).
- Highlight the **benefits** of your service, not just the features.
- Use a **strong call-to-action** (CTA), such as "Schedule Your Inspection Today" or "Get a Free Estimate."

Make sure your ads are visually appealing, using eye-catching images or videos of your team in action or showcasing wildlife problems you've solved. The goal is to compel users to stop scrolling and pay attention to your message.

4. Optimize Your Ad Campaigns Continuously

Social media advertising is not a "set it and forget it" strategy. Regularly monitor your campaigns, keeping an eye on key performance metrics like:

- **Click-through rates (CTR)**: How many people are clicking on your ads?
- **Conversion rates**: How many clicks are turning into leads or customers?
- **Return on ad spend (ROAS)**: Are you generating more revenue than you're spending on ads?

Use this data to tweak your targeting, ad copy, or creative elements to improve results. You may need to test different ad formats, adjust your budget, or refine your audience to get the best outcomes.

5. Ensure Landing Page Optimization

Once users click on your ad, the landing page they arrive at must be optimized to convert them into leads. Create dedicated landing pages tailored to the specific service or offer promoted in your ad. To increase conversion rates:

- Ensure **fast load times**—slow pages can lead to higher bounce rates.
- Use **clear messaging** that aligns with the ad, so users know they're in the right place.
- Include **easy-to-fill forms** for users to request quotes, schedule services, or sign up for more information.

A seamless user experience from ad click to landing page action is key to driving conversions.

6. Manage Your Ad Budget Wisely

It's essential to set a clear and realistic budget for your social media ad campaigns. Start with a small budget and monitor performance closely. Based on the results, you can scale up your investment in ads that perform well or make adjustments to underperforming campaigns. Keep in mind that advertising budgets are fluid, and it's important to adjust your spending based on the performance data and your evolving business goals.

7. Ensure Compliance with Advertising Regulations

Make sure your ads comply with local laws and regulations related to wildlife removal and pest control services. Be familiar with advertising guidelines in your region, including any restrictions on how you can market your services. Ethical advertising practices are essential to maintaining a positive reputation and avoiding legal issues.

CHAPTER 9
Content Marketing

An educated customer is often the best customer, especially when that education comes directly from you. When potential clients trust you as a knowledgeable and reliable source, their confidence in your services improves exponentially. By creating and sharing educational content on your website and social media, you can inform customers about key topics such as your processes, pricing, and service offerings. This type of engagement builds trust and positions your business as an authority, making it easier for prospects to choose you when the need arises.

Content marketing plays a crucial role in this process, especially for wildlife removal and pest control companies. Through well-crafted and informative content, you can attract, engage, and educate your audience while establishing yourself as an expert in the field. The first step is understanding your audience. Identifying their specific needs, concerns, and pain points allows you to tailor your content accordingly. For example, a homeowner dealing with squirrels in the attic will respond well to content that addresses both prevention and removal techniques, while another might be more interested in seasonal pest control tips.

Creating high-quality content is essential. This might include blog posts, articles, infographics, and videos that offer valuable insights into wildlife removal techniques, pest control strategies, and preventive measures. Your content should always be well-researched, accurate, and up-to-date, as this strengthens your credibility and positions your business as a go-to resource in the industry. You're not just answering questions or solving problems; you're showcasing your expertise and dedication to helping your audience.

Search engine optimization (SEO) should not be overlooked when crafting content. By conducting keyword research and incorporating relevant terms into your articles and media, you can ensure your content ranks well in search engine results. Using strategic headings, meta tags, and alt tags boosts your visibility and increases the chances of organic traffic finding its way to your website. This not only helps potential customers discover your content but also draws in those who are specifically searching for services you offer.

Once your content is ready, it's essential to share it across the channels most frequented by your target audience. Your website's blog is an obvious home, but you should also promote your content through social media platforms, email campaigns, and even industry-specific forums or online communities. Each platform offers an opportunity to engage with different segments of your audience, helping to spread your message and drive traffic back to your website.

The primary focus of your content should always be to provide value and education. Rather than pushing overly promotional messages, aim to solve common problems, answer frequently asked questions, and offer practical advice. By educating your audience on wildlife removal techniques or pest control best practices, you'll build trust and credibility over time, which leads to stronger brand authority and increased customer loyalty.

However, the success of your content marketing efforts depends on regularly measuring performance. Key metrics like website traffic, audience engagement, and conversion rates will give you valuable insights into what's working and what's not. By reviewing this data, you can adjust your content strategy to ensure continuous improvement and better outcomes.

Content Marketing Tip: Leveraging AI for Content Creation

In recent months, artificial intelligence (AI) tools, such as OpenAI's ChatGPT, have gained popularity for their ability to assist with content creation. These language models can help generate ideas or draft content quickly, but it's important to remember that AI lacks the deep technical expertise required for accurate wildlife or pest control information. Any content generated by AI should be carefully reviewed and edited to ensure accuracy and relevance.

Rather than viewing AI as a shortcut, think of it as a tool to enhance your writing efficiency. AI can help you produce well-structured, grammatically sound content at a faster pace, but it still requires your guidance. You provide the direction, and the AI assists in speeding up the process, helping you create more content in less time while maintaining control over the messaging and accuracy.

By using a blend of traditional content marketing techniques and modern AI tools, wildlife removal and pest control companies can effectively educate their audience, build trust, and grow their business in a competitive market.

Here are some key tips for effectively utilizing content marketing in your wildlife removal and pest control business:

1. Identify Your Target Audience: Clearly define your target audience, including their interests, preferences, and pain points. Understanding your audience will help you create content that resonates with them and provides value. Tailor your content to address their specific needs and concerns related to wildlife removal and pest control.
2. Create High-Quality Content: Create high-quality and informative content that is relevant to your audience. This can include blog posts, articles, infographics, videos, and other types of content. Provide valuable information about wildlife removal techniques, pest control strategies, prevention tips, and other relevant topics. Make sure your content is well-researched, accurate, and up-to-date to establish your credibility as an expert in the field.
3. Optimize Content for SEO: Optimize your content for search engines to ensure it gets maximum visibility. Conduct keyword research to identify relevant keywords and incorporate them strategically in your content. Use relevant headings, meta tags, and alt tags to optimize your content for search engine optimization (SEO). This will help your content rank higher in search engine results, driving organic traffic to your website.

4. Share Content on Relevant Channels: Share your content on relevant channels where your target audience is active. This can include your website blog, industry-specific forums, online communities, and other platforms where your audience is likely to engage. Use social media, email marketing, and other channels to promote your content and drive traffic to your website.
5. Provide Value and Educate: Focus on providing value to your audience through your content. Educate them about wildlife removal and pest control best practices, tips, and techniques. Avoid overly promotional content and instead focus on solving their problems and addressing their concerns. This will help you build trust and establish yourself as a reliable source of information, leading to increased brand authority and customer loyalty.
6. Measure and Adjust: Regularly measure the performance of your content marketing efforts using relevant metrics such as website traffic, engagement, and conversions. Analyze the data and adjust your content strategy as needed to continuously improve the effectiveness of your content marketing efforts.

Video Marketing

Video marketing offers a powerful way to engage potential customers and showcase your services. Videos demonstrating your expertise, such as a "day in the life" of a wildlife removal technician or customer testimonials, can build trust and provide valuable insights into your work. Explainer videos about how to prevent common wildlife issues or behind-the-scenes looks at your humane removal processes can also resonate well with your

CUSTOMER ATTRACTANT

audience. Video content can be shared across social media, embedded in email marketing campaigns, and featured on your website to boost engagement and conversion rates.

TATE MORGAN

CHAPTER 10
Email Marketing

Email marketing can be an extremely effective tool for wildlife removal and pest control companies to connect with their audience, build relationships, and foster loyalty. It offers a direct line to potential and existing customers, ensuring your services remain top-of-mind while nurturing leads and encouraging repeat business. When executed correctly, email marketing not only helps attract new customers but also plays a crucial role in customer retention, ultimately driving long-term business growth.

Developing an Effective Email Marketing Strategy

The foundation of any successful email marketing campaign begins with building a strong, permission-based email list. This list should consist of individuals who have opted to receive communications from your business, ensuring you're targeting a receptive audience. To encourage sign-ups, offer something of value in exchange for email addresses. This might include pest prevention guides, seasonal tips for wildlife control, exclusive discounts, or access to premium resources such as wildlife identification tools or DIY inspection checklists.

(Users engage with Emails at all times throughout the day, making email marketing one of the strongest brand-building tools)

Once you have built your email list, audience segmentation becomes critical. Segmenting allows you to divide your subscribers into specific groups based on factors such as their location, the type of pests they've dealt with, the services they've used, or even their stage in the customer journey (new lead vs. returning customer). By segmenting your audience, you can tailor your messages to be more personalized and relevant, which increases engagement and conversion rates.

Creating Valuable and Engaging Content

The content you send to your subscribers is the backbone of your email marketing strategy. For pest control and wildlife removal companies, educational content can be particularly valuable. Share **seasonal pest prevention tips**, **wildlife control advice**, and updates on **local pest trends**. For example, an email in the spring might offer tips on preventing squirrel infestations in attics, while a fall email could highlight the importance of checking for rodents as temperatures drop. Positioning your company as a helpful resource builds trust and encourages subscribers to turn to you when they need professional services.

In addition to educational content, promotional elements are essential for driving conversions. Include clear, action-oriented calls-to-action (CTAs) that guide your audience toward the next step, whether it's scheduling an inspection, booking a service, or taking advantage of a limited-time offer. Emails promoting **seasonal discounts**, **new services**, or **free consultations** can be particularly effective in converting leads into customers.

A successful email marketing campaign should balance **informative content** with **promotional offers**. This blend keeps your audience engaged while gently reminding them of the services you provide. Avoid making every email a hard sell; instead, focus on being helpful, with an occasional push toward taking action when the timing is right.

Fostering Customer Relationships Through Email Marketing

Email marketing isn't just about driving immediate sales—it's about building long-term relationships. Regularly staying in touch with customers ensures your business remains top-of-mind when they eventually need wildlife removal or pest control services. Even if they aren't ready to hire you today, receiving helpful content and promotions over time ensures they think of you first when they do have a problem.

You can also use email marketing as a tool to enhance customer retention. For example, sending personalized follow-up emails after a service, offering maintenance tips or reminders for future inspections, and sharing loyalty offers can keep previous customers engaged. Satisfied customers are far more likely to use your services again and refer your company to friends and family.

Encourage referrals through your email campaigns by offering incentives. You could create a referral program where customers receive a discount or a free service after referring someone else to your business. Including a clear and simple referral call-to-action within your emails can generate new leads and expand your customer base through word-of-mouth marketing.

Optimizing Your Email Campaigns for Success

To ensure the success of your email marketing efforts, it's crucial to continually analyze key performance metrics such as open rates, click-through rates, and conversion rates. Monitoring these metrics can help you identify what's working and where adjustments need to be made.

For instance, if your open rates are low, consider experimenting with different subject lines. Test variations that include urgency, questions, or personalization (e.g., using the subscriber's first name) to increase engagement. If you notice that your click-through rates are underperforming, examine your content and

CTAs. Are the emails visually appealing? Is the message clear and concise? Do the links take subscribers to relevant, optimized landing pages?

A/B testing is another valuable strategy for optimizing your email marketing. You can test different subject lines, content formats, email designs, and sending times to discover which combination resonates best with your audience.

Timing is another critical factor in email success. While there's no universal best time to send emails, testing different times and days can reveal when your audience is most likely to open and engage with your content. For example, sending pest control tips early in the week might catch homeowners while they're planning their weekend tasks, while a Friday afternoon email offering a discount for emergency wildlife removal might appeal to those dealing with sudden issues over the weekend.

Leveraging Automation to Streamline Campaigns

Automation is an invaluable tool for streamlining your email marketing efforts. Automated email sequences allow you to nurture leads and maintain customer engagement with minimal manual intervention. For instance, you can set up **welcome emails** for new subscribers, **follow-up sequences** for past customers, or even **automated reminders** for regular pest inspections or maintenance services. Automated drip campaigns can provide a steady flow of useful information to your audience while keeping them engaged with your business over time.

CHAPTER 11
Online Reputation Management

R eputation management refers to the practice of actively monitoring, influencing, and managing the reputation of a business or brand online. It involves managing and shaping the perception of a business among its target audience, customers, and stakeholders.

For wildlife removal and pest control businesses, reputation management can play a crucial role in building trust, credibility, and a positive image among potential customers. A positive online reputation can help establish your business as reliable, trustworthy, and reputable in the eyes of potential customers, leading to increased customer inquiries, bookings, and referrals.

(Positive reviews displayed on a company's website can go a long way for solidifying the customer's decision)

Here are some ways reputation management can help a wildlife removal or pest control business:

1. Online Reviews: Online reviews are a key component of reputation management. Positive reviews on platforms like Google, Yelp, and other relevant review websites can significantly impact the perception of your business. Potential customers often rely on reviews to assess the quality of your services and determine your credibility. Positive reviews can also boost your search engine rankings and online visibility.
2. Brand Monitoring: Monitoring your brand mentions online can help you identify any negative comments, reviews, or feedback about your wildlife removal or pest control business. By actively monitoring and addressing any negative comments or reviews promptly, you can mitigate any potential damage to your reputation and demonstrate your commitment to customer satisfaction.
3. Social Media Management: Social media platforms are a common place for customers to share their experiences and opinions about businesses. Managing your social media accounts and addressing any comments, reviews, or messages in a timely and professional manner can help you maintain a positive reputation and build strong customer relationships.
4. Responding to Feedback: Promptly responding to customer feedback, whether it's positive or negative, shows that you value your customers' opinions and are willing to address any concerns. It also provides an opportunity to showcase your excellent customer service and willingness to resolve any issues, which can help enhance your reputation.

Getting more reviews for your wildlife removal or pest control business:

1. Ask Satisfied Customers: Reach out to satisfied customers and ask them to leave a review on relevant review websites or social media platforms. You can send them a personalized email, include a review request on your invoices or receipts, or simply ask them in person.
2. Make it Easy: Provide clear instructions and links to review websites, making it easy for customers to leave a review. Include direct links on your website, social media profiles, and email signatures to encourage customers to leave reviews.
3. Incentives: Consider offering incentives to customers who leave reviews, such as discounts on future services or small gifts as a token of appreciation. However, be mindful of the ethical and legal implications of offering incentives, and ensure that you comply with the policies of the review websites.
4. Follow-Up: If a customer has expressed satisfaction with your services, follow up with a gentle reminder to leave a review after a few days or weeks. However, avoid being pushy or overly aggressive in seeking reviews, as it can backfire and negatively impact your reputation.

In summary, reputation management plays a crucial role in building and maintaining a positive image for wildlife removal and pest control businesses. By actively monitoring and managing your online reputation, encouraging and responding to customer reviews, and providing excellent customer service, you can enhance your reputation and attract more customers to your business.

CHAPTER 12
Analytics and Reporting

The Power of Marketing Data and Analytics

In today's digital landscape, data is king. It has become an invaluable resource for wildlife removal and pest control companies seeking to advertise their services more effectively. The use of marketing data and analytics allows businesses to better understand their customers, evaluate the performance of their advertising campaigns, and make informed decisions to maximize return on investment (ROI).

Unveiling Customer Insights

At the heart of every successful advertising campaign is a deep understanding of the target audience. With the aid of data analytics, businesses can gain insights into the behaviors, preferences, and needs of their potential customers.

(Tools like Google Analytics help break down how your customers are behaving while on your website)

For instance, data can reveal which services are most sought after at different times of the year, helping businesses tailor their advertising messages to align with seasonal trends. It can also shed light on demographic details such as age, location, or homeownership status, allowing companies to target their advertisements more precisely.

These customer insights can be instrumental in crafting advertising campaigns that resonate with the target audience, thereby increasing engagement and conversions.

Evaluating Advertising Performance

Another significant advantage of marketing data and analytics lies in performance evaluation. Companies can track various metrics related to their advertising campaigns, such as click-through rates, conversion rates, and customer acquisition costs.

This enables businesses to understand which aspects of their advertising campaigns are working and which ones may need improvement. For instance, a high click-through rate but a low conversion rate could indicate that while the advertisements are attracting attention, they are not compelling enough to drive action. Such insights would prompt a reevaluation of the advertising content or the landing page to which the ads are directed.

Informing Decision Making

By revealing what works and what doesn't, marketing data and analytics equip businesses with the knowledge to make informed decisions. They can identify the most effective advertising channels, the optimal times to run their ads, the best geographic regions to target, and the most appealing messaging strategies.

This ability to base decisions on solid data significantly enhances the effectiveness of advertising efforts, ensuring that every dollar spent is directed towards strategies that yield the highest return.

The Analytics Tools You Need

There are several analytics and reporting tools available that can help wildlife removal and pest control companies measure, analyze, and optimize their online performance. These tools provide valuable insights and data that can inform business decisions, identify areas for improvement, and drive more effective marketing strategies. Here are some commonly used tools:

1. Customer Relationship Management (CRM) Software: CRM software is a valuable tool that helps businesses manage interactions with their customers and prospects. It allows you to store customer data, track leads, manage sales pipelines, and automate marketing campaigns. CRM software can help wildlife removal and pest control companies track customer interactions, manage customer inquiries, and streamline sales and marketing efforts.
2. Google Analytics: Google Analytics is a free web analytics tool offered by Google that provides detailed insights into website performance. It helps you track website traffic, user behavior, conversion rates, and other key metrics. Google Analytics can help wildlife removal and pest control companies understand how their website is performing, identify which marketing channels are driving the most traffic and conversions, and optimize their online strategies accordingly.
3. Social Media Analytics Tools: Social media platforms often come with built-in analytics tools that provide data on engagement, reach, and other metrics. For example, Facebook Insights, Twitter Analytics, and LinkedIn Analytics provide insights into the performance of your social media posts, audience demographics, and engagement levels. These tools can help wildlife removal and pest control companies measure the effectiveness of their social media efforts, identify which content resonates with their audience, and refine their social media strategy.
4. Online Review Management Platforms: Online review management platforms, such as Yelp for Business Owners, Google My Business, and other industry-specific review sites, provide analytics and reporting on customer

reviews. These tools allow wildlife removal and pest control companies to monitor and manage their online reviews, track customer feedback, and respond to reviews in a timely and effective manner.

5. Heat Mapping Tools: Heat mapping tools, such as Hotjar, provide visual insights into how users interact with your website. They generate heat maps that highlight areas of your website that receive the most engagement or attention, as well as areas that users may be missing. This can help wildlife removal and pest control companies optimize their website design, content placement, and call-to-action buttons to improve user experience and increase conversions.

CHAPTER 13

Empowering Traditional Marketing with Digital Strategies

Digital marketing tools can be effectively used to complement and enhance traditional marketing strategies for wildlife removal and pest control businesses. By integrating digital marketing tools into traditional marketing efforts, businesses can leverage the power of online channels to increase brand visibility, reach, and customer engagement. Here are a few ways in which digital marketing tools can improve the effectiveness of traditional marketing strategies:

1. Targeted Advertising: Digital marketing tools such as Google Ads, social media advertising, and email marketing allow wildlife removal and pest control businesses to target their audience with precision. Through targeted advertising, businesses can deliver their message to specific demographics, geographic locations, or user interests, ensuring that their marketing efforts reach the right audience at the right time. This can complement

traditional marketing efforts such as print ads, billboards, or direct mail by amplifying the reach and impact of these traditional channels.

2. Call Tracking: One of the most important digital tools you can use to amplify your traditional marketing strategies is Call Tracking. One of the biggest challenges when running television, direct mail, or out-of-home advertising (like billboards and local sponsorships) is a lack of awareness around what is bringing you the best results. With call tracking phone numbers (provided by services such as CallRail), you can utilize a different phone number for each advertising campaign or placement. Within your call tracking dashboard, you can see exactly which number has been dialed and how many times. This helps demystify the effectiveness of your offline marketing channels.

3. Enhanced Brand Visibility: Digital marketing tools such as search engine optimization (SEO) and social media marketing can significantly boost the online visibility of wildlife removal and pest control businesses. A strong online presence can lead to higher organic search rankings, increased social media followers, and a larger online community. This increased brand visibility can complement traditional marketing efforts by creating multiple touchpoints with potential customers, reinforcing brand awareness, and driving more leads and referrals.

4. Data-Driven Decision Making: Digital marketing tools provide valuable data and insights that can inform marketing strategies and optimize traditional marketing efforts. Tools like Google Analytics, CRM software, and social media analytics allow businesses to track and analyze data related to customer behavior, engagement,

and conversions. This data can help wildlife removal and pest control businesses identify which traditional marketing channels or campaigns are most effective, and make data-driven decisions to optimize their marketing budget, messaging, and targeting.
5. Improved Customer Relationship Management (CRM): CRM software, a digital marketing tool, can help wildlife removal and pest control businesses streamline their customer relationship management efforts. CRM software allows businesses to centralize customer data, track interactions, and automate marketing campaigns. By leveraging CRM, businesses can enhance their traditional marketing strategies by staying organized, managing customer inquiries efficiently, and maintaining effective communication with prospects and customers.
6. Amplified Word-of-Mouth Marketing: Digital marketing tools such as online reviews, social media sharing, and email marketing can amplify word-of-mouth marketing efforts for wildlife removal and pest control businesses. Positive online reviews, social media shares, and email referrals can encourage and influence others to engage with the business, leading to increased brand advocacy and referrals. This can complement traditional word-of-mouth marketing efforts, such as customer testimonials, referrals, and reviews, by extending the reach and impact of positive customer experiences.

CHAPTER 14

Future Trends in Digital Marketing for Wildlife Removal and Pest Control Companies

While the concepts in this book are considered evergreen, the digital marketing landscape is constantly changing. There are constantly innovations in marketing tools, as well as changes to the platforms on which we advertise day-to-day. Today, you might find Facebook Ads to be the most effective, but changes in laws, technology, or user behavior could force this to change.

(We don't actually see Facebook going anywhere anytime soon. This is purely an example. However, the consideration is still important).

As we look to the future of digital marketing, it's impossible to know exactly what will bring tomorrow's best results, but there are some trends to keep in mind as we move into the future.

1. Personal Privacy: Personal privacy is becoming a bigger concern by the day. New laws are constantly being drafted that limit what advertisers and digital platforms can do with customer data. It's important to remember that behind every online interaction, there is a real-life person. How did your advertising use their data? Will they continue to be comfortable with that use in the future? If the answer is no, then your advertising strategies may be subject to change.
2. Artificial Intelligence: As major tech companies, such as Meta, Google, and Microsoft, develop their own artificial intelligence tools, search results will almost certainly shift. Rather than searches that return a list of results, AI search engines may provide a conversational written answer first. While we don't know exactly how this will affect digital marketing strategies, it's safe to assume that we should strive to be as helpful and as truthful as possible online. When these AI tools train, they scour the internet for accurate information then share that information with searchers. You will have a significant leg up in the future of search if your website provides accurate and relevant information for users.
3. Social Media Shifts: Social media platforms don't last forever. As much as they'd like us to believe they are *forever companies*, the risk of deplatforming always exists. From government regulation to shifting demographics, the social media platforms you use today will almost certainly not be the platforms you use in 10 years. Geocities disappeared. Myspace disappeared. AOL Chatrooms disappeared. The list goes on and on. It's important to explore new social media platforms as they emerge so you can continue to be where your potential customers are.

CHAPTER 15
Conclusion

As wildlife removal and pest control experts, you know that the competition in the industry is fierce. In today's digital age, having a robust online presence is crucial to stay ahead and succeed. That's where digital marketing comes in.

Throughout this book, we have explored the ins and outs of digital marketing specifically tailored to your industry. From search engine optimization (SEO) to Google Ads, social media marketing to content marketing, email marketing to reputation management, we have covered it all. By utilizing these digital marketing strategies, you can effectively reach your target audience, build brand visibility, engage with customers, and generate leads and sales.

As a wildlife removal or pest control business owner, you understand the importance of staying relevant and adapting to the changing landscape of the digital world. Incorporating digital marketing into your overall marketing strategy can be the key to achieving success in today's competitive market. By leveraging digital marketing tools, such as customer relationship management (CRM) systems and Google Analytics, you can gain valuable insights into customer behavior, measure the effectiveness of your marketing efforts, and make data-driven decisions to optimize your strategies.

Digital marketing can enhance your traditional marketing efforts. By integrating your digital and traditional marketing strategies, you can create a cohesive and comprehensive approach that maximizes your reach and impact. For example, utilizing digital advertising to drive traffic to your website or social media pages, and then engaging with your audience through content marketing, email marketing, and reputation management can strengthen your overall marketing efforts and boost your business results.

As wildlife removal and pest control business owners, digital marketing can be a game-changer for your business. By staying updated with the latest digital marketing trends, technologies, and best practices, you can effectively connect with your audience, drive business growth, and achieve your marketing goals. The insights and strategies outlined in this book are designed to help you leverage digital marketing to gain a competitive edge, increase online visibility, and generate tangible results for your business.

Wishing you success in your digital marketing endeavors!

Sincerely, Tate Morgan, and the LeadSquirrel Team

APPENDIX
Tools and Resources

This appendix provides a list of useful tools, resources, and websites to help you effectively implement digital marketing strategies for your wildlife removal and pest control business. These resources cover various aspects of digital marketing, from SEO to social media management, email marketing, and customer relationship management (CRM).

1. SEO Tools

- **Google Keyword Planner**: Free tool to discover relevant keywords for your SEO campaigns. It helps you find search volumes and competition levels.
- **Ahrefs**: A comprehensive SEO tool that provides insights into keyword rankings, backlinks, and competitor analysis.
- **SEMrush**: All-in-one tool that helps with keyword research, SEO audits, content marketing, and more.
- **Moz**: Provides SEO tracking tools, link building insights, and keyword research capabilities.

- **Yoast SEO** (for WordPress users): A plugin that helps optimize content for search engines.

2. Social Media Management Tools

- **Hootsuite**: A platform to schedule and manage social media posts across multiple platforms.
- **Buffer**: Helps you plan and publish content on social media. Also provides performance analytics.
- **Canva**: Easy-to-use graphic design tool to create engaging social media graphics.
- **Sprout Social**: Provides social media management, reporting, and listening features to track engagement and monitor trends.

3. Content Marketing Tools

- **BuzzSumo**: Helps you find trending topics and popular content in your industry to inspire your blog or social media posts.
- **Grammarly**: An AI-powered writing assistant that helps with spelling, grammar, and tone, ensuring your content is clear and professional.
- **Notion AI**: A tool that helps generate content ideas and even draft content quickly.
- **Descript**: Video and audio editing software that simplifies the process of creating marketing videos or podcasts.

4. PPC and Advertising Tools

- **Google Ads**: Essential for creating pay-per-click (PPC) campaigns to target potential customers through Google Search and Display Network.

- **Facebook Ads Manager**: Helps you create and manage ad campaigns for Facebook and Instagram.
- **Nextdoor Advertising**: A platform to target local communities with ads relevant to specific neighborhoods.
- **CallRail**: A call tracking tool that helps track which marketing channels are driving phone calls to your business.

5. Email Marketing Tools

- **Mailchimp**: Offers email marketing automation, templates, and audience segmentation tools for targeted email campaigns.
- **Constant Contact**: An email marketing service that helps with building email lists, creating templates, and tracking campaign performance.
- **ActiveCampaign**: Provides advanced email automation features, including CRM integration and targeted email workflows.
- **HubSpot**: A full-featured marketing automation platform, offering CRM, email marketing, and lead nurturing solutions.

6. Online Reputation Management Tools

- **Google My Business**: Essential for managing your Google Business Profile, encouraging customer reviews, and improving local SEO.
- **Yelp for Business Owners**: Helps manage your Yelp listing and respond to customer reviews.

- **BirdEye**: A tool to monitor and manage online reviews across various platforms, helping improve your business's online reputation.
- **Trustpilot**: Allows businesses to collect customer reviews and ratings to build credibility and trust.

7. Analytics and Reporting Tools

- **Google Analytics**: The go-to tool for tracking website performance, understanding user behavior, and measuring marketing campaign success.
- **Hotjar**: Provides heatmaps and session recordings to understand how visitors interact with your website.
- **Microsoft Clarity**: A free heatmapping and user session recording tool that helps improve user experience on your website.
- **Data Studio (Google)**: Helps create visually engaging reports by connecting with Google Analytics, Google Ads, and other data sources.

8. CRM Tools

- **Salesforce**: A powerful CRM platform that helps manage customer relationships, track sales, and automate marketing efforts.
- **Zoho CRM**: A user-friendly CRM with features for managing leads, automating tasks, and tracking sales pipelines.
- **HubSpot CRM**: A free CRM that integrates with marketing automation tools to track customer interactions and manage leads.

- **Pipedrive**: A sales-focused CRM that helps wildlife removal and pest control companies manage leads, track deals, and streamline communications.

Further Learning and Industry Resources

- **Search Engine Land**: A trusted source for the latest SEO, PPC, and digital marketing news and strategies.
- **LeadSquirrel Blog (https://animalcontrolmarketing.com)**: Provides practical tips and guides on SEO, PPC, content marketing, and social media advertising specifically for pest control & wildlife removal companies.
- **Social Media Examiner**: A resource for mastering social media marketing and staying informed on new trends and strategies.
- **HubSpot Academy**: Free courses on digital marketing, SEO, email marketing, content creation, and more.

By utilizing these tools and staying informed through these resources, you can continuously improve your digital marketing efforts and stay ahead of the competition in the wildlife removal and pest control industry.